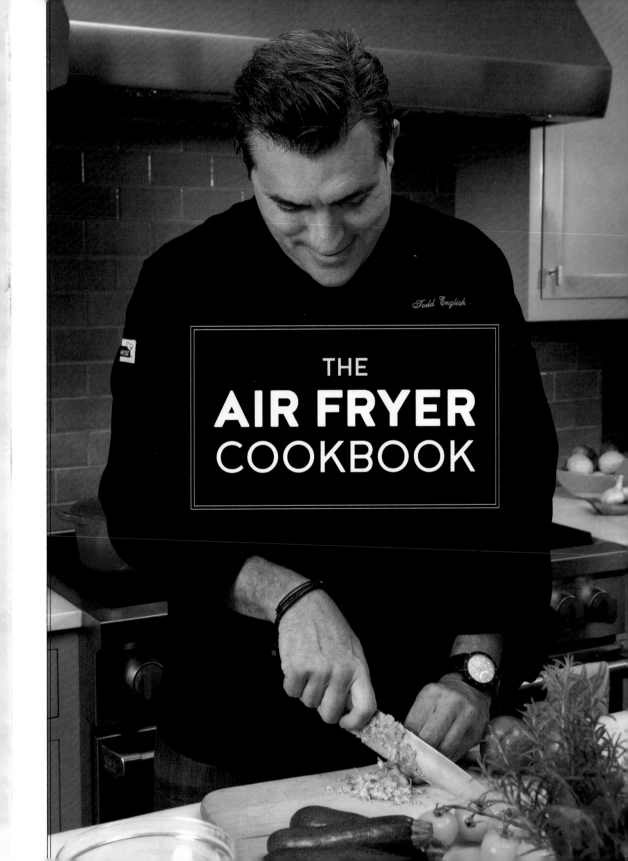

THE
AIR FRYER
COOKBOOK

THE AIR FRYER COOKBOOK

Deep-Fried Flavor Made Easy, Without All the Fat!

TODD ENGLISH

ST. MARTIN'S CASTLE POINT

NEW YORK

www.stmartins.com

Photography by Allan Penn

The Library of Congress Cataloging-in-Publication Data is available upon request

ISBN 978-1-250-09614-2 (paper over board)
ISBN 978-1-250-10491-5 (signed edition)

Our books may be purchased in bulk for promotional, educational, or business use. Please contact your local bookseller or the Macmillan Corporate and Premium Sales Department at (800) 221-7945, extension 5442, or by e-mail at MacmillanSpecialMarkets@macmillan.com.

First Edition: December 2015

10 9 8 7 6 5

CONTENTS

INTRODUCTION

For me, cooking has always been a family affair—from growing up watching my mother and grandmother making fresh pasta, to experimenting to see what foods my kids would actually eat, to enjoying the happiness I feel today when I'm in my kitchen surrounded by family and friends.

When cooking for your family, you have a lot of things you have to balance at once. You want the food to taste delicious, of course—but that's just the beginning! You also want to have variation in your weekly menu, while still keeping any picky eaters happy with their favorites. Scheduling can be a nightmare—when will everyone be home from practice and other activities, and when will *you* find the time not only to eat, but to clean up the kitchen? And, of course, you have to do all of this while still trying to keep the food healthy!

That's why I really love cooking with an air fryer. Tasty food that's packed with flavor *and* satisfies your urge for CRUNCH? Check. Lots of easy ways to make crowd-pleasers with a twist like Mac 'n' Cheese Bites (page 9) and Chipotle Chicken Fingers (page 61)? Check, check. Quicker than just about any other appliance in your kitchen, with virtually no cleanup? Check, check, check! And the kicker of course is that it's one of the healthiest ways to prepare foods, because you're using hot air to cook your food rather than a lot of fattening, artery-clogging oils. Not only that, since you can make French fries better than the fast-food restaurant can (page 108), no more succumbing to your kids' pleas to take a trip through the drive-thru.

Anyone who has a kitchen that's become the family hub knows that it can get crowded in there. Air fryers don't take up that much space, and they're simple. There aren't any complicated bells and whistles—just set the time and temperature, and you're done. In the next section, I'll give you a full overview of how to use your air fryer—but it's short, because there isn't much to learn!

Beginning with some amazing appetizers to get you warmed up, I'll share with you recipes my family and I have had fun making with this awesome tool. You can do a lot more with your air fryer than just fry things: You can grill, roast, and even bake (yes, there's a desserts chapter). The recipes are fast—you'll be hard-pressed to find one that takes longer than half an hour to prepare. Best of all, they're healthy. While some use oil in tiny amounts to get a crispier crust, many use no oil or fat at all—making them lower in fat, cholesterol, and lots of other stuff that's bad for our bodies.

Because the air fryer is so easy to use, you don't have to worry about method. So focus on your ingredients instead! Buying the freshest possible fruits, vegetables, meat, fish, and even bread will have a huge impact on the taste of your meals. Go organic when you can, and make sure to visit your local farmers' market!

I hope this book will teach you some great new recipes to cook with my favorite kitchen gadget, allow you to revisit some tasty fried snacks that had become "guilt" foods, and inspire your family's kitchen! That reminds me . . . I could be eating some air-fried Eggplant Parm Chips right now (you can find the recipe on page 104).

Happy Cooking!

Todd English

HOW TO USE YOUR AIR FRYER

THE BASICS

Air fryers work by rapid air cooking—evenly circulating hot air to cook fresh or frozen foods, which gives them the same crunchy bite and moist interiors produced by conventional deep fryers, all while never submerging them in cooking oils or fats. In other words, the air *is* the oil!

I love air frying so much that I've developed my own Todd English air fryer. But you can use this book with any basket air fryer.

PARTS OF THE AIR FRYER

Inside the air fryer unit is a removable heating chamber and a cooking basket. To take the cooking basket out of the heating chamber, just press the release button and lift it out.

Many air fryers also come with a removable rack, used for keeping meats off the bottom of the basket, or for steaming items with a little liquid underneath. If you're lucky, you have the Todd English Air Fryer, which also has a pizza pan that can be used for cooking pizza (naturally) and as a baking tin. If you don't have a pizza pan especially for your air fryer, you can use a glass, silicone, or metal oven-safe dish instead. No matter which you use, place it in the basket before cooking. (In order for the air fryer to operate, the heating chamber—with the cooking basket in it—must be secured in the air fryer.)

GETTING STARTED

To cook items in your air fryer, it's really as easy as throwing them in the basket and selecting the time and temperature! Some air fryers have presets (for instance, on my air fryer, you can select "Bacon," and it will automatically cook for 15 minutes at 370° F). But if your air fryer doesn't, or you're cooking something there isn't a preset for, I've included a handy chart on pages 144–145 of common foods and their cook times and temps. Spraying a little nonstick cooking spray on the items first is usually a good idea, as it will help them crisp up. When cooking items that you want crunchy on all sides, it's also usually a good idea to pull out the basket halfway and flip the items, or simply shake the basket to toss them around a bit.

PREHEATING

It only takes about 3 minutes for an air fryer to preheat. In fact, if you want, you can simply add 3 minutes to the cook time and throw everything in without pre-heating. I told you it was easy!

AIR FRYER SAFETY TIPS

Air fryers are powerful machines, so make sure you stay safe.

• Air fryers get HOT! Especially if you've added oil or steaming liquid to the pan. While your food cooks, liquids will accumulate in the cooking chamber, so always use caution when removing the basket. After the cooking cycle is complete, the basket will be very hot! So after removing it, don't put it down anywhere that can't handle heat—it can burn your counter.

• Before cooking anything, make sure all the ingredients are inside the air fryer basket, to prevent any contact with the heating element.

• During the cooking cycle, hot air/steam is released through the air outlets. So keep your hands and face away from them, and don't place anything on top of the appliance during operation or otherwise cover the air inlets or outlets.

Be safe! Don't use the appliance if there is any damage to the plug, electrical cord, or any other parts. Don't use the air fryer (or plug it in) with wet hands, and don't leave it unattended while it's in operation. Unplug the fryer after you're done using it.

TAKING CARE OF YOUR AIR FRYER

WHERE TO KEEP YOUR AIR FRYER

I like to keep my air fryer handy on the kitchen counter, but wherever you end up using yours, make sure it's a flat, even, and stable surface. Make sure to leave at least 5 inches of free space around the back, sides, and top of the appliance for a clear air flow.

CLEANING YOUR AIR FRYER

Always wait 30 minutes for the air fryer to cool down before handling or cleaning it. You should clean the air fryer after every use by wiping down the outside with a moist cloth; cleaning the heating chamber and cooking basket by hand with soap and water in the kitchen sink; and cleaning the inside of the appliance with a damp (wrung-out), nonabrasive sponge, wiping away any food debris and grease. Never clean any part of an air fryer with metal kitchen utensils or abrasive cleaning materials because they can damage the nonstick coating. If there's debris stuck to the basket or bottom of the pan, simply soak it in hot, soapy water for about 10 minutes to loosen it up before cleaning. If necessary, you can clean the heating element with a wet cleaning brush to remove debris (again, just make sure it's completely cool first!).

AIR FRYER COOKING TIPS

Air fryers are really easy to use, but here are some tips for making sure you get the most out of them!

• Any food that can be cooked in a microwave or oven can be cooked in an air fryer.

• To give food a crispy texture, spray cooking oil or nonstick spray over the ingredients before adding them to the basket. Alternatively, you can add a small amount (3–4 tablespoons) of oil to the pan before cooking. (Never overfill, as this will damage the air fryer.)

• Smaller ingredients usually require a slightly shorter cooking time than larger ingredients. Shaking smaller ingredients halfway during the cooking time ensures they'll be evenly cooked.

• To steam food, add a small amount (3–4 tablespoons) of liquid, such as water or broth, to the pan after adding the ingredients. (Never overfill, as this will damage the air fryer.)

• You can also use an air fryer to reheat food by setting the temperature to 300° F for up to 10 minutes.

• See the Quick-Reference Cooking Chart on pages 144–145 for a cheat sheet on how long to cook most foods.

APPETIZERS AND SMALL BITES

THAI SPRING ROLLS

CHEESY RICE BALLS

SPINACH-FETA ARANCINI

MAC 'N' CHEESE BITES

GAME DAY MOZZARELLA STICKS

RICOTTA CHEESE BOMBS

MASHED POTATO CROQUETTES

SNAPPY SESAME TRIANGLES

FRIED DUCK WONTONS

MARYLAND CRAB CAKES

FRESH-CAUGHT SALMON CROQUETTES

FRIED BUFFALO WINGS

HONEY-GARLIC WINGS

JALAPEÑO PARTY POPPERS

FRIED RAVIOLI POPPERS

COUNTRY CORN FRITTERS

ZUCCHINI FRITTERS

"CHEATER" CROQUETTES

THAI SPRING ROLLS

Even if you're a novice at detecting flavors, ginger is unmissable. It's a must-add for me in any Thai spring roll because just the smell of it makes you want to take a bite.

4 ounces boneless chicken breast, cooked and roughly chopped

1 celery stalk, roughly chopped

1 medium carrot, peeled and roughly chopped

½ cup baby bella mushrooms, chopped

½ teaspoon freshly grated ginger

1 garlic clove, minced

¼ teaspoon freshly ground black pepper

1 tablespoon soy sauce

1 tablespoon hoisin sauce

1 teaspoon lime juice

1 large egg

1 teaspoon cornstarch

8–10 refrigerated spring roll wrappers, or frozen spring roll wrappers, thawed

Olive oil cooking spray

① Place the chicken, celery, carrot, and mushrooms in a food processor and pulse until shredded. Add the ginger, garlic, and pepper and pulse until well mixed, about 1 minute. Stir in the soy sauce, hoisin sauce, and lime juice.

② In a separate bowl, whisk together the egg and the cornstarch. The resulting paste will become the "glue" that holds each wrapper together.

③ Place each wrapper on a clean, dry surface, with a corner facing you. Spoon approximately 1 tablespoon of the filling onto a wrapper, near the bottom corner. Then lift this corner up and roll until you use up half of the wrapper. Fold the sides in, then continue rolling up, tucking the edges in as you go, until you use up the wrapper.

④ Dab a small amount of the cornstarch-egg mixture onto the remaining corner with your fingertip, then press it against the rest of the spring roll to seal. Repeat with remaining wrappers and filling.

⑤ Spray the spring rolls liberally with cooking spray and place them seam-side down in the cooking basket, leaving space between each one.

⑥ Air fry in batches at 390° F until golden and crunchy, about 6 minutes.

◯ Makes 4 servings

CHEESY RICE BALLS

I won't hold it against you if you buy the risotto for these delicious rice balls pre-made at a restaurant or Italian specialty store, but making it at home is easier than you think. It requires that you spend a little time in front of the stove, but to get the creamy texture of great risotto, the Arborio rice really does the work for you—just make sure to use warm broth or it will come out too starchy.

RISOTTO

1 tablespoon unsalted butter

½ medium Spanish onion, finely chopped

2 garlic cloves, minced

½ cup dry white wine

1 cup Arborio rice

4 cups low-sodium chicken broth, warmed, plus additional as needed

¼ cup freshly grated Parmesan cheese

salt to taste

¼ teaspoon freshly ground black pepper

RICE BALLS

2 cups risotto

½ cup Gruyère cheese, cut into ½-inch cubes

1 cup all-purpose flour

2 large eggs, beaten

1 cup Panko Breadcrumbs (page 142)

Olive oil cooking spray

TO MAKE THE RISOTTO:

① Melt the butter in a large saucepan over medium heat. Then add the onion and garlic, stirring well and cooking about 5–6 minutes, until the ingredients are softened and golden.

② Stir in the wine and cook another 4 minutes, until the wine is nearly evaporated. Then add the rice and stir until well coated.

③ Add ½ cup of the broth and stir well, scraping the bottom and sides of the pan, and cook until it has been absorbed by the rice. Continue adding the broth, ½ cup at a time as the liquid is absorbed, stirring well after each addition. If rice is still tough, add additional broth until tender.

④ Stir in the Parmesan, salt, and pepper and remove from the heat. To accelerate cooling, you can remove the risotto from the saucepan and place in a bowl.

TO MAKE THE RICE BALLS:

① When the risotto has cooled, scoop approximately 2 tablespoons into the palm of your hand. Place a cube of Gruyère in the middle, then roll into a ball, making sure to close the cheese completely into the ball. Repeat with remaining risotto.

② Roll each of the balls in flour, then dip into the beaten egg, then roll into the breadcrumbs, coating evenly.

③ Spray each ball with cooking spray before adding to the basket. Leave space between rice balls. Air fry at 400° F for 10 minutes per batch, or until golden.

○ Makes 4–6 servings

SPINACH-FETA ARANCINI

We have "rice balls," the Italians have *arancini*, so named because they look like *arancia* (Italian for "orange"). For the risotto, use the recipe from the Cheesy Rice Balls (pages 4–5), or use the shortest-grain rice you can find and add an extra tablespoon of water when preparing it to increase the stickiness.

1 tablespoon olive oil

1 large shallot, chopped

1 (10 ounce) package frozen chopped spinach, thawed and drained

½ cup crumbled feta cheese

2 cups risotto (or short-grain white rice), cooked and well cooled

1 cup all-purpose flour

2 large eggs, beaten

1 cup Panko Breadcrumbs (page 142)

Olive oil cooking spray

① Heat the olive oil in a medium saucepan. Add the shallots and sauté until golden.

② Add the spinach and sauté with the shallots until the flavors mix, about 2–3 minutes. Drain excess liquid. Stir in the feta and set the mixture aside to cool.

③ Scoop approximately 2 tablespoons of the risotto onto the palm of your hand and flatten.

④ Add about a teaspoon of the spinach-feta filling, then carefully pack into a ball shape. Repeat with the remaining risotto and filling.

⑤ Roll each of the balls in the flour, then dip into the beaten egg, then roll into the breadcrumbs, coating evenly.

⑥ Spray each ball with cooking spray before adding to the basket. Air fry at 400° F for 10 minutes per batch, or until golden.

◯ Makes 4–6 servings

MAC 'N' CHEESE BITES

These crunchy balls of goodness make homemade mac 'n' cheese even better—and they'll keep you from eating the entire pan at once. Amazingly, the air fryer not only lets you quickly cook the bites, it provides a lightning-fast way to make the mac 'n' cheese itself.

Olive oil cooking spray

1½ cups elbow macaroni, uncooked

1 cup chicken broth

½ cup heavy cream

¾ cup shredded Cheddar cheese

½ cup freshly shredded mozzarella cheese

¼ cup freshly grated Parmesan cheese

Salt and pepper, to taste

2 large eggs, beaten

1 cup Basic Homemade Breadcrumbs (page 142)

① Spray a cake pan with cooking spray and add the macaroni, broth, cream, cheeses, and salt and pepper. Mix the ingredients together and place the pan in the center of the basket.

② Air fry for 30 minutes at 350° F, or until the mac 'n' cheese is bubbling and golden brown. Set aside to cool.

③ When cool, scoop out approximately 2 tablespoons of the mac 'n' cheese and roll into a ball shape. Set aside on a cookie sheet. Repeat until you've run out of mac 'n' cheese. Place the pan in the refrigerator until the balls are firm, approximately 4 hours.

④ Remove the balls from the refrigerator and dip each into the beaten egg, then roll into the breadcrumbs, coating evenly.

⑤ Spray each ball with cooking spray before adding to the basket. Air fry at 400° F for 10 minutes per batch, or until golden.

◯ Makes 4–6 servings

GAME DAY MOZZARELLA STICKS

If the game is on, I'm eating mozzarella sticks! Even though mozzarella sticks are some of the tastiest things in the world, they're really easy to make with an air fryer and some string cheese. They go well with my Marinara Dipping Sauce (page 131).

1 (12 ounce) package mozzarella string cheese
2 cups Italian-seasoned Breadcrumbs (page 143)
¼ cup freshly grated Parmesan cheese
¼ cup all-purpose flour
2 large eggs, beaten
Olive oil cooking spray

① Remove the cheese from the individually wrapped packages and stack on a cutting board. With a sharp knife, slice the sticks in half, or thirds, depending on the size you like. Place the sticks on a cookie sheet covered in parchment paper and place in the freezer, covered with plastic wrap, for 2 hours.

② Mix together the breadcrumbs and Parmesan cheese.

③ Immediately upon removing the sticks from the freezer, roll them first in the flour, then the beaten eggs, then the breadcrumb-Parmesan mixture. As you prepare them, place them back on the cookie sheet you used to freeze them until they're all ready.

④ Place the sticks in the air fryer basket, making sure they don't touch. Spray the sticks with cooking spray all around, then place the basket into the air fryer.

⑤ Air fry for 3 minutes at 400° F, then remove and carefully flip. Air fry for an additional 3–4 minutes, or until golden.

○ Makes 4–6 servings

RICOTTA CHEESE BOMBS

These Ricotta Cheese Bombs are an explosion of herbed Italian flavor in every bite.

1 cup ricotta cheese

2 tablespoons all-purpose flour

½ teaspoon dried thyme

½ teaspoon dried rosemary, crushed

½ teaspoon dried basil

½ teaspoon kosher salt

¼ teaspoon freshly ground pepper

2 large eggs, beaten, divided

1 cup Basic Homemade Breadcrumbs (page 142)

Olive oil cooking spray

① In a medium bowl, combine the ricotta, flour, thyme, rosemary, basil, salt, pepper, and half of the beaten eggs. Stir until well mixed.

② Scoop approximately 1 tablespoon of the mixture into the palm of your hand and roll into a ball. Repeat with the remaining mixture.

③ Dip each of the balls into the remaining beaten egg, then into the breadcrumbs, coating evenly.

④ Place the balls on a cookie sheet and refrigerate for 1 hour.

⑤ Spray the ricotta balls with olive oil cooking spray before adding to the basket, being careful not to overcrowd it. Air fry in batches at 400° F until golden, about 8–9 minutes.

○ Makes 4–6 servings

MASHED POTATO CROQUETTES

Every family has a great mashed potatoes recipe—just not all of them have an awesome way to turn leftover mashed potatoes into crunchy, bite-sized bits of joy. I've given you a basic mashed potatoes recipe below, but feel free to use your family's favorite. Just don't omit the egg yolk and flour when you make the croquettes, as they're the "glue" that holds the breadcrumb coating onto the potatoes.

MASHED POTATOES

2 medium russet potatoes, peeled and cubed

1 tablespoon unsalted butter

¼ cup whole milk

¼ teaspoon kosher salt

½ cup freshly grated Parmesan cheese

CROQUETTES

mashed potatoes

yolk of 1 large egg

2 tablespoons all-purpose flour, plus extra for rolling

2 tablespoons finely chopped fresh chives

⅛ teaspoon freshly ground black pepper

2 large eggs, beaten

½ cup Panko Breadcrumbs (page 142)

Olive oil cooking spray

TO MAKE THE MASHED POTATOES:

① Boil the potatoes in salted water until soft, about 15 minutes. Drain.

② Add the butter, milk, salt, and Parmesan cheese. With a masher, ricer, or fork, mash just until well blended and there are minimal lumps. Set aside to cool.

TO MAKE THE CROQUETTES:

① Add the egg yolk, flour, chives, and pepper to the cooled potatoes.

② Scoop out approximately 1 tablespoon of the mixture and roll into a ball shape. Repeat with the remaining mixture.

③ Roll each croquette in flour to coat, then dip into the beaten egg, then roll into the breadcrumbs, coating evenly.

④ Spray each ball with cooking spray before adding to the basket. Air fry (in batches if necessary) at 390° F for 8 minutes, or until golden.

○ Makes 4 servings

SNAPPY SESAME TRIANGLES

Sesame seeds might be one of the most underrated seeds, and they really shine in these crispy little toasts. Use whatever veggies you have left over from stir-fry night, or just cook up a package of mixed vegetables from the freezer.

1 cup mixed vegetables (such as carrots, baby corn, and green beans), cooked and finely chopped

2 garlic cloves, minced

1 tablespoon cornstarch

1 teaspoon sesame oil

¼ teaspoon salt

Sesame seeds, to coat (about 6 tablespoons)

6 slices white bread, cut into quarters on the diagonal

Canola oil cooking spray

① Combine the first 5 ingredients in a food processor and pulse into a fine paste.

② Pour out the sesame seeds onto a plate or clean work surface.

③ Spread the vegetable mixture on one side of each of the slices of bread. Press the bread into the seeds, vegetable side down, so the seeds cling to the vegetable mixture. Spray the seeded sides of the triangles with cooking spray.

④ Air fry at 390° F until golden brown, about 5–8 minutes.

○ Makes 4–6 servings

FRIED DUCK WONTONS

Sometimes I can't stop craving Chinese food, and that's when I'm glad I have an air fryer. It makes perfect wontons that are crisp but not too greasy. These fancy versions contain smoked duck breast, but you can make them with chicken breast and they're almost as delicious.

1 stalk celery, chopped

¼ medium red onion, chopped

2 teaspoons freshly grated ginger

1½ tablespoons soy sauce

2 teaspoons sesame oil

1 teaspoon chili oil

1 tablespoon rice vinegar

3–4 ounces smoked duck breast

1 (12 ounce) package wonton skins

Cooking spray

① Combine all the ingredients in a food processor except the wonton skins and cooking spray. Pulse into a fine paste.

② Lay out the wonton skins on a clean work surface. Add about a teaspoon of the filling to the middle of each skin.

③ To fold the wontons, using your fingertips, wet two edges with a small amount of water, then fold over on the diagonal. Press edges to seal. Now pull up the two corners of the "triangle" and press to seal, forming a dumpling shape. Repeat for rest of wontons.

④ Spray the air fryer basket and wontons with cooking spray. Air fry in batches at 390° F until crispy, about 6 minutes. Shake once during cooking time.

◯ Makes approximately 24 wontons

MARYLAND CRAB CAKES

What makes a crab cake a Maryland Crab Cake? Some would say it's Maryland crabs! But I think crab cakes can be called Maryland as long as they're made with Old Bay seasoning—an earthy spice mixture that originated in Maryland especially to season seafood. Serve these on buns with a salad and they're whole meals unto themselves. They also pair well with the Homemade Tarter Sauce (page 137).

1 tablespoon olive oil

1 small onion, finely chopped

1 stalk celery, finely chopped

1 small red pepper, finely chopped

2 tablespoons unsalted butter

1 tablespoon mayonnaise

½ teaspoon Old Bay seasoning

1 teaspoon fresh lemon juice

1 teaspoon hot sauce (optional)

1 teaspoon Worcestershire sauce

8 ounces lump crab meat

1 large egg, beaten

1 cup crushed butter crackers (like Ritz or Town House)

Olive oil cooking spray

① Heat the olive oil in a saucepan over medium heat. Add the onions, celery, and red pepper and heat, stirring occasionally, until soft, about 3 minutes.

② Add in the butter, mayonnaise, and Old Bay, and cook until the liquid evaporates, about 3–5 more minutes. Remove mixture to a bowl and set aside to cool—about half an hour on the counter or 10 minutes in the refrigerator.

③ Once mixture has cooled, add the lemon juice, hot sauce (if using), Worcestershire sauce, lump crab meat, and egg, and gently fold in with a wooden spoon, rubber spatula, or your hands.

④ Place the crushed crackers in a shallow bowl and set aside.

⑤ For smaller crab cakes, shape approximately 2 tablespoons of the mixture into a patty. For larger patties, use ¼ cup of the mixture per patty. Press the patty into the cracker crumbs to coat. Repeat until you've used all of the crab mixture.

⑥ Place a batch of crab cakes in the air fryer basket, ensuring they are not touching, and spray with cooking spray. Fry in batches at 400° F until golden brown, about 8 minutes.

○ Makes 2–4 servings

FRESH-CAUGHT SALMON CROQUETTES

Don't be tempted to use canned salmon in these croquettes, which are much tastier if you use fresh. In fact, air frying is one of my favorite ways to cook salmon that's moist inside and crispy outside—and the combination of textures is one of the things that elevates these croquettes to the next level. Serve with one of the sauces on pages 129–140.

1 (8 ounce) salmon fillet, cut in half

2 tablespoons extra virgin olive oil, divided

¼ teaspoon kosher salt

⅛ teaspoon freshly ground black pepper

2 tablespoons finely chopped fresh dill

3 shallots, finely chopped

1 large egg, beaten

½ cup Basic Homemade Breadcrumbs (page 142)

1 tablespoon fresh lemon juice

Olive oil cooking spray

① Coat the salmon with 1 tablespoon of the olive oil, place in the air fryer basket and sprinkle with salt, pepper, and dill. Air fry at 370° F for 10 minutes, until cooked through and flaky. Flip halfway through cooking time.

② While the salmon is cooking, heat the remaining 1 tablespoon of oil in a small saucepan over medium heat and add the shallots. Cook until tender, stirring occasionally, approximately 2–3 minutes. Remove from heat and set aside.

③ When the salmon is done cooking, let it sit for 3–5 minutes, then mash with a fork in a bowl and let cool, covered, for 15–20 minutes.

④ In a large bowl, combine the egg, shallots, and salmon. Mix well. Add lemon juice to breadcrumbs. Fold in breadcrumbs with your hands.

⑤ Scoop about 2 tablespoons of the mixture into your palm and form balls, flattening them if you prefer patties.

⑥ Spray with cooking spray and place in the air fryer basket, making sure to leave space between each one. Air fry in batches at 400° F until golden, about 8 minutes.

◯ Makes 3–4 servings

FRIED BUFFALO WINGS

Nothing is more satisfying with a frothy beer than a pile of hot, spicy buffalo wings. Some people will tell you to slather on the sauce before you cook the wings, but they're wrong—it can make them soggy. Fry the wings first to give them an irresistible crunch, then cover them in as much spicy sauce as you can handle. Serve with blue cheese dressing, celery, and carrot sticks, if desired.

6 bone-in chicken wings

4 tablespoons unsalted butter, melted

4 tablespoons hot sauce

1 teaspoon cider vinegar

1 teaspoon soy sauce

1 teaspoon ketchup

① Rinse the wings and pat dry. Section the wings in three parts, discarding the tips. Place the midsections and drumettes in the basket and air fry at 400° F until cooked through, about 25 minutes. Shake the basket 2–3 times during cooking to flip the wings.

② While the chicken is cooking, prepare the sauce: In a large bowl, whisk together the melted butter, hot sauce, cider vinegar, soy sauce, and ketchup.

③ When wings finish cooking, add them to bowl and toss with sauce to coat.

◯ Makes 2 servings

HONEY-GARLIC WINGS

These Asian-inspired wings are literally finger-licking good. The sweet yet spicy sauce is super sticky, thanks to the honey. This recipe is a great choice for those times when you crave chicken wings, but not the heat of buffalo sauce.

6 bone-in chicken wings

½ cup soy sauce

2 garlic cloves, minced

4 tablespoons fresh ginger, shredded

⅓ cup light brown sugar

⅓ cup honey

Pinch of pepper

Approximately 3 tablespoons cornstarch, as thickener

① Rinse the wings and pat dry. Place in the air fryer basket and air fry at 400° F, until cooked through, about 25 minutes. Shake the basket 2–3 times during cook time to flip the wings.

② While the wings are cooking, prepare the sauce: In a medium saucepan, over medium heat, mix together the soy sauce, garlic, ginger, brown sugar, honey, and pepper, stirring continuously.

③ As the sugar melts and the honey thins, begin adding the cornstarch a pinch at a time. Keep stirring in the cornstarch until you arrive at the desired consistency for your sauce, then remove from heat.

④ When the wings are done cooking, place them in a large bowl. Pour the sauce over the wings and toss to coat.

◯ Makes 2 servings

JALAPEÑO PARTY POPPERS

Some people like to make their jalapeño poppers with cream cheese, and some like to make them with Cheddar. With these flavorful poppers, I bring them together for a cream cheese–Cheddar party! Make sure to keep the stems intact on these bad boys as they make great "holders" when eating.

1 (8 ounce) package cream cheese, softened

1 cup shredded Cheddar cheese

2 tablespoons fresh cilantro, chopped

1 tablespoon chipotle or other hot sauce

24 small jalapeño chilies, cut in half lengthwise and seeded

2 large eggs, beaten

1 cup Basic Homemade Breadcrumbs (page 142)

Olive or canola oil cooking spray

Salt and pepper

① In a large bowl, mix together the cream cheese, Cheddar cheese, cilantro, and hot sauce.

② Spoon cheese and cilantro mixture into 1 jalapeño half and top with an empty half. Push together; the cream cheese will act as "glue." Repeat with the rest of the jalapeños.

③ Dip each of the peppers into the beaten egg, then into the breadcrumbs, coating evenly.

④ When all the peppers have been coated, refrigerate for at least 1 hour and as long as overnight.

⑤ Spray the poppers with oil and place the first batch in the cooking basket. Sprinkle with salt and pepper. Air fry in batches at 400° F until golden brown, about 12 minutes.

◯ Makes 4 servings

FRIED RAVIOLI POPPERS

The secret to making perfect fried ravioli in the air fryer is freezing the ravioli beforehand, so in this instance I might even recommend just grabbing a bag of your favorite frozen brand at the grocery store . . . even though the Italian in me says you should make them from scratch with homemade semolina dough and fill them with seasonal fillings such as roasted butternut squash and sage, or finely chopped shrimp with parsley and Parmesan cheese. It's up to you!

24 cheese ravioli, frozen

2 cups all-purpose flour

3 large eggs, beaten

2 cups Basic Homemade Breadcrumbs (page 142)

Olive oil cooking spray

① Dredge each frozen piece of ravioli in flour, then dip into the beaten egg, then into the breadcrumbs, pressing on each side to coat evenly. Spray them with olive oil, then place them in the basket, leaving space between each one.

② Air fry in batches at 380° F until golden brown, about 20 minutes. Serve with my Marinara Dipping Sauce (page 131).

◯ Makes 6–8 servings

COUNTRY CORN FRITTERS

The sweetness of summer corn shines in these simple-yet-delicious country classics.

> **1 tablespoon olive oil**
> **2 shallots, finely chopped**
> **2 cups fresh corn removed from the cob (from about 4 ears)**
> **1 large egg, beaten**
> **½ cup 2% milk**
> **2 tablespoons butter, melted**
> **½ cup freshly grated Parmesan cheese**
> **½ cup cornmeal**
> **½ cup all-purpose flour**
> **½ teaspoon kosher salt**
> **¼ teaspoon freshly ground black pepper**
> **Canola oil cooking spray**

① In a saucepan, heat the olive oil over medium heat, then add the shallots. Sauté until soft, approximately 2–3 minutes, stirring occasionally.

② Add the corn and toss together, sautéing an additional 1–2 minutes. Remove from heat and set aside.

③ In a large mixing bowl, combine the egg, milk, butter and Parmesan cheese. Then add the corn-shallots mixture, cornmeal, flour, salt, and pepper. Toss well to combine and let sit for 10–15 minutes to thicken.

④ Scoop approximately 2 tablespoons of the mixture into the palm of your hand and shape into either a ball or pancake, depending on your preference. Repeat until you use up the remaining mixture.

⑤ Spray the fritters with canola oil cooking spray and add to the basket. Be sure not to overcrowd or allow fritters to touch.

⑥ Air fry in batches at 400° F until golden, about 10 minutes.

◯ Makes 3–4 servings

ZUCCHINI FRITTERS

If zucchini has never really done much for you, you haven't met these zucchini fritters. Grate the zucchini with a box grater, then layer on the flavor with garlic, scallions, and Parmesan cheese, and make it all pop with a crunchy air-fried crust.

1 medium zucchini, peeled and grated

¼ cup freshly grated Parmesan cheese

1 large egg, beaten

½ teaspoon kosher salt

¼ teaspoon freshly ground black pepper

1 garlic clove, minced

1 large scallion, white and green parts, finely chopped

½ cup Italian-seasoned Breadcrumbs (page 143)

Olive oil cooking spray

① In a medium bowl, combine the zucchini, Parmesan, egg, salt, and pepper and mix until combined. Mix in the garlic and chopped scallion, then fold in the breadcrumbs.

② Scoop about 2 tablespoons of the mixture into the palm of your hand. Roll into a ball, then flatten into a pancake about ¼-inch thick. Repeat with remaining mixture.

③ Place fritters in the basket of the air fryer, leaving space between each one. Spray on all sides with olive oil cooking spray.

④ Air fry at 390° F until golden, about 7 minutes.

○ Makes 2–3 servings

"CHEATER" CROQUETTES

Cauliflower is a secret weapon for anyone wanting to indulge in appetizers while still watching their weight. I boil the cauliflower before I make the croquettes so that it's almost the exact same consistency as potatoes. Parmesan is not only my favorite cheese, but it also has fewer calories than most other cheeses—so you don't even need to feel guilty about that part of these appetizing bites.

2 cups cauliflower florets

1 cup seasoned Panko Breadcrumbs (page 142)

¼ cup freshly grated Parmesan cheese

1 large egg, beaten

Olive oil cooking spray

① Blanch the cauliflower by heating in boiling water for 2–3 minutes, then immediately rinsing with cold water to stop the cooking process. Place in a bowl and let cool for 5 minutes.

② Toss the breadcrumbs with the Parmesan cheese.

③ Dip each of the florets into the beaten egg, then into the breadcrumb mixture, coating evenly.

④ Place the florets into the basket of the air fryer, leaving space between each one. Spray with olive oil cooking spray, then place the basket into the air fryer.

⑤ Air fry in batches at 400° F until golden, about 10 minutes.

◯ Makes 3–4 servings

MAIN
DISHES

FRIED VEGGIE TEMPURA • LIGHTNING-FAST FRITTATA

CHEESE-STUFFED MUSHROOMS • FALAFEL WITH FLAIR

TODD ENGLISH PIZZA • PORTOBELLO SPINACH PIZZA

EGGPLANT BOATS • GARLIC FRIED SHRIMP

QUINOA-CRUSTED SHRIMP • COCONUT SHRIMP

SPICY SCALLOPS • LONDON FRIED FISH

CRISPY SNAPPER WITH LIME BUTTER

SALMON TERIYAKI

LAMB EMPANADAS

CRISPY CHINESE DUCK • CHIPOTLE CHICKEN FINGERS

BALSAMIC BARBECUE CHICKEN

CHICKEN SATAY WITH THAI PEANUT SAUCE

COUNTRY-FRIED CHICKEN • SPICY AFRICAN CHICKEN

SESAME-GINGER FRIED PORK

COUNTRY FRIED PORK CHOPS

DIJON-GARLIC PORK TENDERLOIN

SMOKEHOUSE RIBS WITH HOMEMADE BBQ SAUCE

SPICY FRIED MEATBALLS • BAD-A** SKIRT STEAK

FRIED VEGGIE TEMPURA

Even though sushi might be the star at many Japanese restaurants, I'm a sucker for tempura, the Japanese equivalent to America's obsession with fried food. This Japanese-style batter is lighter than its American equivalent, with soda water used to add air to the batter. Give it a try and see what you think.

½ cup cornstarch

½ cup all-purpose flour

1 large egg, lightly beaten

¾ cup cold soda water

1 small Japanese eggplant, sliced into ¼-inch discs

1 small sweet potato, sliced into ¼-inch discs

1 red pepper, seeded and sliced into ¼-inch-long strips

1 cup broccoli florets

1 cup Panko Breadcrumbs (page 142)

Canola oil cooking spray

Kosher salt and freshly ground black pepper, to taste

① In a large bowl, fold together the cornstarch, flour, egg, and soda water. The batter will be slightly lumpy. Let sit, covered, for 30 minutes.

② Dip each vegetable into the batter, shaking off any excess, then dredge in the breadcrumbs, pressing on each side to coat evenly.

③ Place veggies in basket with space between each one. Spray on all sides with oil. Air fry in batches at 400° F until golden, about 7 minutes.

④ Season with salt and pepper before serving.

○ Makes 4–6 servings

LIGHTNING-FAST FRITTATA

A frittata seems like an undertaking, especially when it's for breakfast and you haven't even finished your coffee yet. But an air-fried frittata is quick—less than 10 minutes from start to finish! Whip up this personal-sized one for somebody special and you're sure to impress.

2 cherry tomatoes, sliced

2 large eggs

1 tablespoon freshly grated Parmesan cheese

2 tablespoons 2% milk

⅛ teaspoon kosher salt

⅛ teaspoon freshly ground black pepper

Canola oil cooking spray

¼ cup baby spinach, roughly chopped

① Lay the tomato slices on a paper towel to absorb excess liquid.

② In a medium bowl, whisk together the eggs, Parmesan cheese, milk, salt, and pepper. Spray the air fryer baking pan with canola oil and place it in the basket. Pour the egg mixture into the pan, then delicately fold in the spinach and tomatoes.

③ Air fry at 400° F until cooked through, about 5 minutes. Serve warm.

◯ Makes 1 serving (or 2 small servings)

CHEESE-STUFFED MUSHROOMS

I love meat, but these mushroom cap sandwiches taste so beefy they're the next best thing. The Muenster and Cheddar cheeses pack in even more flavor, but these palate-pleasers somehow still remain delicate.

1 tablespoon extra virgin olive oil

8 large portobello mushroom caps, stems and gills removed

4 ounces Muenster cheese, shredded

4 ounces sharp Cheddar cheese, shredded

1 cup all-purpose flour

2 large eggs, beaten

1 cup Panko Breadcrumbs (page 142)

Olive oil cooking spray

① Heat the olive oil in a large saucepan over medium-high heat. Add the mushroom caps and sear on each side, about 4–5 minutes per side. Remove from pan and blot with paper towels to remove excess moisture.

② Fill 1 mushroom cap with ¼ of the Muenster and Cheddar cheeses, then top with an additional cap. Repeat with remaining caps and cheese.

③ Take a mushroom stack and dredge it in the flour. Then dip it into the beaten egg, then into the breadcrumbs, coating evenly. Repeat with remaining mushroom stacks and spray all with olive oil cooking spray.

④ Place 1 or 2 mushroom stacks in the air fryer. Air fry at 380° F until cheese is melted, about 6 minutes, flipping halfway through. Repeat with remaining mushroom stacks.

◯ Makes 4 servings

FALAFEL WITH FLAIR

Hummus has gotten more and more popular in recent years, and falafel is its crunchy cousin. Made mostly with ground chickpeas, falafel also boasts the green goodness of parsley and cilantro, both of which pair flawlessly with the zesty flavors of garlic, onion, and red pepper flakes.

1 (8 ounce) can chickpeas

2 garlic cloves

1 small Spanish onion, quartered

½ tablespoon fresh Italian flat-leaf parsley leaves

1 tablespoon fresh cilantro leaves

¼ teaspoon kosher salt

Pinch of crushed red pepper flakes

2 tablespoons olive oil

¼ cup all-purpose flour

⅛ teaspoon baking powder

Canola oil cooking spray

① Add all the ingredients except the cooking spray to your food processor. Pulse until combined (it should be similar to the texture of cooked oatmeal), about 2–3 minutes. Cover and refrigerate for 1–2 hours.

② Scoop approximately 2 tablespoons of the mixture into the palm of your hand and shape into a ball. Repeat with remaining mixture.

③ Spray the falafel balls with canola oil cooking spray and place in the basket, leaving space between each one. Air fry in batches at 390° F until golden, about 10 minutes.

◯ Makes 2–4 servings

TODD ENGLISH PIZZA

If you love a crispy pizza crust, you'll love how my personal-sized pizzas come out when you bake them in an air fryer. If you don't have time to make your own dough, stop at your local pizza place and ask to buy some of theirs. And, of course, add your favorite pizza toppings.

DOUGH

1 (.25 ounce) packet active dry yeast

¼ cup granulated sugar

1⅔ cups warm (100° F–110° F) water, divided

¾ cup extra virgin olive oil

1 tablespoon kosher salt

5 cups all-purpose flour, plus more for dusting

PIZZAS

1 (28 ounce) can whole peeled tomatoes, drained

2 tablespoons extra virgin olive oil

½ teaspoon dried oregano

1 teaspoon kosher salt

½ teaspoon freshly ground black pepper

6 ounces fresh mozzarella cheese, torn into 6 pieces

6–12 fresh basil leaves

TO MAKE THE DOUGH:

① In a medium bowl, combine the yeast, sugar, and 1 cup of the water and stir until the sugar dissolves.

② Pour into the bowl of an electric stand mixer fit with a dough hook attachment. Add the remaining water, olive oil, and salt. Add the flour and beat at low speed until dough comes together and is smooth, about 10 minutes.

③ Cover the bowl of dough with lightly greased plastic wrap, and let it rise in a warm place free from drafts until doubled in bulk, about 1½ hours.

④ Punch down the dough and turn out onto a lightly floured surface. Divide into 6 portions for individual pizzas. For each pizza, place a dough round in the pizza pan and fold any excess inward, pressing into the crust.

TO MAKE THE PIZZAS:

① In a large bowl, crush the tomatoes repeatedly with your hands until they reach your desired consistency. Stir in the olive oil, oregano, salt, and pepper.

② Spread tomato mixture over each dough round, leaving a border around the edge. Top each with 1 ounce of the mozzarella cheese.

③ Air fry in batches at 400° F until crust is golden brown and cheese is melted, about 10 minutes. Top each pie with 1–2 leaves of basil.

◯ Makes 3–4 servings

PORTOBELLO SPINACH PIZZA

This recipe uses mushroom caps in lieu of a flour-based crust for a super healthy alternative to traditional pizza, but the rich heartiness of the portobello will make you feel like you're indulging.

8 ounces fresh spinach

1 garlic clove, minced

4 tablespoons olive oil, divided

2 medium tomatoes, diced

½ cup fresh basil, chopped

Salt and pepper, to taste

1 tablespoon red wine vinegar

4 large portobello mushrooms with stems and gills removed

½ cup Parmesan cheese, grated

1½ cups mozzarella cheese, grated

① Sauté the spinach with the garlic and 2 tablespoons of the olive oil until wilted and set aside. Combine the tomatoes, basil, salt, pepper, remaining 2 tablespoons of olive oil, and red wine vinegar. Divide the tomato-basil mixture into the portobello caps. Top with the spinach, followed by the Parmesan and mozzarella cheeses.

② Air fry at 380° F until the mushrooms are tender and the cheese begins to brown, about 6 minutes.

◯ Makes 4 servings

EGGPLANT BOATS

In this variation on Eggplant Parmesan, I make the eggplant into crispy "boats" that hold all the rest of the classic Italian toppings. It's impossible to eat just one of these, so make a batch.

2 small eggplants

¼ cup extra virgin olive oil

1 teaspoon kosher salt

½ teaspoon freshly ground black pepper

1 cup Italian-seasoned Breadcrumbs (page 143)

1 cup Marinara Dipping Sauce (see page 131)

8 slices fresh mozzarella cheese

½ cup freshly grated Parmesan cheese

¼ cup chopped fresh basil

① Rinse the eggplants and pat dry. Do not peel. Slice off the tops, then slice each eggplant in half lengthwise. These are the "boats."

② Coat the outside of each eggplant boat with olive oil and sprinkle with salt and pepper. Sprinkle ¼ cup of the breadcrumbs onto each section.

③ Line the pan of your air fryer with aluminum foil. Place the eggplant boats in the pan, leaving space between each one, and air fry in batches at 390° F for 10 minutes.

④ Remove from the air fryer and spoon marinara on top of each of the boats, followed by 2 slices of mozzarella for each (cut the slices in half to more efficiently cover the eggplant, if desired). Sprinkle each boat with Parmesan cheese.

⑤ Place boats back inside the air fryer until the cheese melts, an additional 5–7 minutes. Sprinkle with the chopped basil.

○ Makes 4 servings

GARLIC FRIED SHRIMP

I love the sweet, briny taste of fresh shrimp, and the simple garlic egg wash used to coat them before air frying in this recipe lends just enough flavor to give them a kick without overpowering them. Meanwhile, air frying means you don't get the greasy aftertaste you often get with fried shrimp.

2 large eggs

3 garlic cloves, minced

1 teaspoon sea salt

¼ teaspoon black pepper

1 pound large shrimp, peeled and deveined

1 cup all-purpose flour

2 cups cornmeal

Olive oil cooking spray

① In a medium bowl, whisk together the eggs, garlic, salt, and pepper.

② Dredge each piece of shrimp in the flour, then dip in the seasoned egg mixture, then roll in the cornmeal until evenly coated.

③ Place coated shrimp in the basket of the air fryer, leaving space between each one. Spray on all sides with olive oil.

④ Air fry in batches at 440° F until crispy, about 10 minutes.

○ Makes 4–6 servings

QUINOA-CRUSTED SHRIMP

You've probably been hearing a lot about the health benefits of quinoa lately, but what you might not know is that it's easy to prepare—and delicious. I crisp it up in this take on crunchy air-fried shrimp.

½ cup all-purpose flour

½ teaspoon ground cumin

½ teaspoon sweet paprika

¾ teaspoon garlic powder

½ teaspoon onion powder

¼ teaspoon sea salt

⅛ teaspoon freshly ground black pepper

1 pound medium shrimp, peeled and deveined

2 large eggs, beaten

1 cup raw quinoa

Olive oil cooking spray

① In a medium bowl, combine the flour, cumin, paprika, garlic powder, onion powder, salt, and pepper.

② Dredge each piece of shrimp in the flour mixture, then dip in the egg, then roll in the quinoa until evenly coated.

③ Place the shrimp in the basket of the air fryer, leaving space between each one. Spray on all sides with olive oil.

④ Air fry in batches at 440° F until crispy, about 10 minutes.

○ Makes 4–6 servings

COCONUT SHRIMP

It may surprise you that coconut and shrimp taste like they were meant for each other. The bigger surprise in this recipe is breading these air-fried bits of awesomeness with crumbs from the bottom of your cornflakes box. They add the perfect sweet-yet-hearty crunch that sends these shrimp over the edge.

2 large eggs

1 tablespoon water

1 cup sweetened coconut flakes

⅔ cup crumbs from cornflakes cereal

1 teaspoon sea salt

1 pound large shrimp, peeled and deveined, but with tails still attached

1 cup cornstarch

Olive oil cooking spray

① In a shallow bowl, beat together the eggs and the water.

② In a separate bowl, combine the coconut flakes, cornflake crumbs, and salt.

③ Dredge each piece of shrimp in cornstarch, then dip in the egg, then roll in the coconut-cornflake mixture until evenly coated.

④ Place the shrimp in the basket of the air fryer, leaving space between each one. Spray on all sides with olive oil.

⑤ Air fry in batches at 400° F until crispy, about 6 minutes.

○ Makes 4–6 servings

SPICY SCALLOPS

Zesty, spicy, and fresh, these breaded scallops are crispy on the outside and tender on the inside. Serve as a main dish or as an impressive hors d'oeuvre.

1 cup Basic Homemade Breadcrumbs (page 142)

1 teaspoon lemon zest

1 teaspoon chili powder

1 teaspoon paprika

1 teaspoon celery salt

Salt and black pepper, to taste

1 egg

1 tablespoon favorite hot sauce

1 pound sea scallops

① Combine the dry ingredients in a bowl and set aside. In a separate bowl, combine the egg and the hot sauce. Dredge each scallop in the egg mixture, then coat thoroughly in the breadcrumb mixture. Air fry at 400° F until golden brown, about 7 minutes.

◯ Makes 4 servings

LONDON FRIED FISH

You might think these fried fillets are just big fish sticks, but they're actually seri-ous street food. Fish 'n' chips are to the Brits what a late-night slice of pizza is to us Americans. Just pair these with a generous portion of Steakhouse Fries (page 110) or Better-than-Fast-Food Fries (page 108), then wrap in paper and sprinkle with malt vinegar for the authentic fish 'n' chips experience.

1 pound sole fillets

½ cup all-purpose flour

2 large eggs, beaten

½ cup Basic Homemade Breadcrumbs (page 142)

1 teaspoon sea salt

1 teaspoon freshly ground black pepper

Olive oil cooking spray

① Slice the sole fillets lengthwise into l-inch wide strips.

② Dredge each strip in the flour, coating on each side. Dip into the beaten egg, then press each side into the breadcrumbs, coating evenly.

③ Place the fish strips into the air fryer, leaving space between each one. Sprinkle with salt and pepper. Spray with cooking spray.

④ Air fry in batches at 400° F until golden brown, about 15 minutes.

○ Makes 4 servings

CRISPY SNAPPER WITH LIME BUTTER

Lime butter is an ideal companion for this delectable fish with a crispy, crunchy outside and a light, flaky interior. The citrus brings out the snapper's natural flavor, while the butter adds a layer of richness that makes the time from serving to forks clattering onto empty plates about 10 minutes flat.

1 pound snapper fillets, cut into 4-ounce fillets

1 tablespoon extra virgin olive oil

½ teaspoon sea salt

¼ teaspoon freshly ground black pepper

½ stick salted butter, melted

2 tablespoons chopped red onion

1 lime, zested and juiced

Lime slices, for garnish (optional)

① Brush the snapper fillets with the olive oil and sprinkle with the salt and pepper. In 2 batches, air fry at 370° F until fish is crisp and flakes with a fork, about 10 minutes, flipping halfway through cooking time.

② Combine the butter, onion, and lime zest and juice.

③ Pour the lime-butter sauce over the top of the fish fillets and garnish with lime slices, if desired.

○ Makes 4 servings

SALMON TERIYAKI

Salmon teriyaki is a popular takeout dish, but instead of spending the money, make it the right way at home. Air frying gives salmon a satisfying, crispy shell while still keeping it moist and tender on the inside—something your local delivery joint will have a lot of trouble matching. Meanwhile, homemade teriyaki is easy to make with ingredients you might already have on hand.

¼ cup sesame oil

¼ cup fresh lemon juice

¼ cup soy sauce

2 tablespoons brown sugar

1 teaspoon freshly grated ginger

1 garlic clove, minced

2 8-ounce salmon steaks

① In a large bowl, whisk together all of the ingredients except the salmon.

② Add the salmon steaks and gently toss to coat. Cover the bowl with plastic wrap and refrigerate for at least 2 hours. Remove from refrigerator and let the fish come to room temperature before cooking.

③ Place the salmon steaks on the rack in the basket and air fry at 390° F until fish is crisp and flakes with a fork, about 10 minutes.

◯ Makes 2 servings

LAMB EMPANADAS

Because they're so easy, flavorful, and filling, these mini meat pies are a staple in Spain and Portugal. They're perfect served with a simple green salad, but you can also make smaller empanadas to turn them into party food.

1 tablespoon olive oil

1 large shallot, finely chopped

1 garlic clove, minced

1 teaspoon dried rosemary, crushed

1 pound ground lamb

Kosher salt and freshly ground black pepper, to taste

1 tablespoon fresh lemon juice

1 sheet refrigerated or frozen puff pastry, thawed

1 large egg, beaten, divided

① Heat the olive oil in a saucepan over medium heat. Add the shallots and cook, stirring occasionally, about 2 minutes. Add the garlic and rosemary and stir until the shallots and garlic are soft, about 30 seconds more.

② Add the ground lamb and stir to mix with the other ingredients. Cook until browned, stirring occasionally, about 10 minutes.

③ Remove from heat and drain. Add salt, pepper, and lemon juice and stir to combine. Set aside to cool.

④ While lamb is cooling, lay out the sheet of puff pastry dough. Using a 3-inch biscuit cutter, cut circles into the pastry.

⑤ Spoon approximately 1 tablespoon of the lamb mixture onto the bottom half of each dough circle, leaving a border of ⅛-inch along the edge. For each empanada, using the tip of your finger or a brush, apply some of the beaten egg to the bottom edge, then fold over the top half of the dough circle. Press the edges together with the tines of a fork.

⑥ Cover the empanadas with plastic wrap and refrigerate for 20 minutes.

⑦ When you're ready for frying, place the empanadas in the cooking basket, leaving space between each one. Brush with the remaining egg.

⑧ Air fry at 390° F until golden brown and crispy, about 12 minutes.

◯ Makes 2-4 servings

CRISPY CHINESE DUCK

Duck is ideal for air frying since the fattiness of the duck means you don't have to add oils. When I think of duck, I usually think of Asian flavors, since they pair perfectly with this meaty yet delicate fowl. The spice rub in this recipe is my version of Chinese five spice powder—use the store-bought version instead and you have a dinner that takes about 3 seconds to prepare!

3 tablespoons cinnamon

2 teaspoons anise seeds

1½ teaspoons fennel seeds

¾ teaspoon ground cloves

1 teaspoon kosher salt

1½ teaspoons freshly ground black pepper

2 duck legs

1 teaspoon chopped Thai basil

① In a small bowl, combine the cinnamon, anise, fennel, cloves, salt, and pepper.

② Rinse the duck legs and pat dry. Trim off any excess fat that hangs over the edge of the meat and use a paring knife to cut several small slits in the skin and fat on the surface of the leg.

③ Coat the legs with the spice rub, rubbing it into the meat with your fingers.

④ Air fry at 340° F for 30 minutes, then increase temperature to 400° F and air fry until cooked through and skin is crispy, about 5 minutes more. If necessary, drain off excess fat into a glass jar or tin midway through the cooking process. Sprinkle with the basil before serving.

○ Makes 2 servings

CHIPOTLE CHICKEN FINGERS

Crunchy, spicy, and melt-in-your-mouth delicious: Do you need anything more? The pecan takes the coating on these simple chicken fingers to a whole new level when it comes to texture and taste, while the chipotle satisfies your spice craving in all the right ways.

½ cup pecans

¼ cup Panko or Basic Homemade Breadcrumbs (page 142)

Zest of 1 orange

½ teaspoon kosher salt

1 large egg

1 tablespoon sauce from a can of chipotle chili peppers in adobo

1 pound white-meat chicken, sliced into "finger" strips

1 cup flour

Canola oil cooking spray

① In a food processor, combine the pecans, breadcrumbs, orange zest, and salt. Pulse until fine.

② In a separate bowl, whisk together the egg and adobo sauce.

③ Dip each of the chicken pieces into the flour, then the egg mixture, then press each side into the pecan-chipotle mixture to coat evenly.

④ Place the chicken fingers in the basket, leaving space between each one, and spray on all sides with canola oil.

⑤ Air fry in batches at 400° F until golden, about 13 minutes, flipping halfway through cooking time.

◯ Makes 2–4 servings

BALSAMIC BARBECUE CHICKEN

Southern barbecue meets my Italian roots in the piquant blend of sweet and sharp in the sauce that tops this simple chicken.

5 tablespoons balsamic vinegar

5 tablespoons brown sugar

3 tablespoons extra virgin olive oil

2 teaspoons Dijon mustard

2 garlic cloves, minced

1 tablespoon finely chopped onion

Kosher salt and freshly ground black pepper, to taste

4 boneless, skinless chicken thighs

① In a large bowl, mix all the ingredients together except the chicken. Let sit, covered, for at least 1 hour.

② Add the chicken to the sauce and toss well to coat thoroughly.

③ Place the chicken on a rack in the air fryer, leaving space between each piece.

④ Air fry in batches at 380° F until cooked through, about 15 minutes.

◯ Makes 2–4 servings

CHICKEN SATAY
WITH THAI PEANUT SAUCE

If you've never had peanut sauce, a staple of Thai and Malaysian cooking, you'll be stunned at how ordinary peanut butter can be transformed into a savory sauce that pairs excellently with chicken. This simple version tastes best when the chicken is allowed to marinate overnight, but it takes only minute to prepare when it's time to cook.

CHICKEN SATAY

3 tablespoons freshly ground or natural-style peanut butter

½ cup soy sauce

½ cup pineapple juice

2 garlic cloves, minced

1 tablespoon freshly grated ginger

1 pound boneless, skinless chicken breasts or tenderloins, pounded to ¼-inch thickness

PEANUT SAUCE

¾ cup freshly ground or natural-style peanut butter

3 tablespoons hoisin sauce

Juice of 1 lime

3 tablespoons soy sauce

2¼ teaspoons chili-garlic (sriracha) sauce

1 garlic clove, minced

¼ cup water (or more)

TO MAKE THE CHICKEN SATAY:

① In a large bowl, combine the first five chicken satay ingredients and whisk until smooth. Add the chicken and toss well to thoroughly coat. Cover and refrigerate for at least 2 hours, but preferably overnight.

② Remove the chicken from the marinade and blot the excess marinade with a paper towel. Thread the chicken onto skewers and place in the air fryer basket, leaving space between each one.

③ Air fry in batches at 400° F until cooked through, about 10 minutes. Serve with Peanut Sauce (see below).

○ Makes 4 servings

TO MAKE THE PEANUT SAUCE:
① Add all of the peanut sauce ingredients to a food processor and blend until smooth, adding more water to thin, as desired.

COUNTRY-FRIED CHICKEN

Break your addiction to fried chicken from the fast-food joint with this Southern-inspired recipe that not only tastes better, but is healthier for you, too.

1 tablespoon garlic powder

1 tablespoon sweet paprika

1 tablespoon chili powder

½–1 tablespoon cayenne pepper

1½ tablespoons kosher salt, divided

1 tablespoon + 1 teaspoon freshly ground black pepper, divided

10 pieces of chicken (I like thighs, but you can use split breasts, wings, or drumsticks, too)

3 large eggs

¾ cup buttermilk

¼ cup water

1 cup all-purpose flour

1 cup cornstarch

2 cups Basic Homemade Breadcrumbs (page 142)

Canola oil cooking spray

① In a large bowl, combine the garlic powder, paprika, chili powder, cayenne pepper, and 1 tablespoon each of the salt and pepper. Add the chicken pieces and toss to coat. Cover and refrigerate overnight.

② In a shallow bowl, beat together the eggs, buttermilk, and water.

③ In a separate shallow bowl, combine the flour, cornstarch, ½ tablespoon of salt, and 1 teaspoon of pepper. Put the breadcrumbs in another bowl.

④ Dip each piece of the chicken into the flour mixture, then the buttermilk mixture, then the breadcrumbs. Spray on all sides with canola oil. Place in basket, leaving room between each piece.

⑤ Air fry in batches at 370° F until cooked through and crispy, about 25 minutes, flipping halfway through cooking time.

○ Makes 4–6 servings

SPICY AFRICAN CHICKEN

I'm not kidding when I say my life was never the same again once I tasted berbere on a trip to the Atlas Mountains in Morocco. Native to Ethiopia, this spice blend was like nothing I had ever tasted before. It's made from local herbs and spices, but this is a close approximation. Save the extra for later in an airtight container, and make sure to use a tiny bit of cooking oil in the air fryer since this is a dry rub.

BERBERE SPICE RUB

3 tablespoons smoked paprika

1 tablespoon crushed red pepper

1 tablespoon ground ginger

2 teaspoons cumin seeds

1 teaspoon ground turmeric

1 teaspoon kosher salt

1 teaspoon fenugreek seeds

1 teaspoon coriander seeds

1 teaspoon ground cardamom

½ teaspoon ground cinnamon

½ teaspoon whole allspice

½ teaspoon black peppercorns

8 whole cloves

CHICKEN

4 boneless, skinless chicken thighs

Canola oil cooking spray

TO MAKE THE SPICE RUB:

① Warm a small saucepan over medium-high heat and add all of the spice rub ingredients. Toast the spices, stirring constantly for approximately 1–2 minutes. Remove from heat as soon as they start to toast (they will become nutty and aromatic)—be careful not to burn them.

② Pour the mixture into a bowl and allow to cool for 10–15 minutes. Once cool, place in a food processor and pulse until fine, about 1 minute.

TO MAKE THE CHICKEN:

① Coat each chicken thigh with about 2 teaspoons of the spice rub, rubbing the mixture into the chicken with your fingers.

② Spray the chicken pieces on all sides with canola oil, then place on a rack in the air fryer. Air fry at 380° F until cooked through, about 25–30 minutes. Flip halfway through cooking time.

◯ Makes 2–4 servings

SESAME-GINGER FRIED PORK

Nothing's better than fried pork, and in this recipe it's balanced with the flavors of sesame and ginger and placed atop a bed of spinach, making sure you get your greens, too! If you don't like your pork spicy, just scale down the amount of hot sauce in the marinade.

SESAME-GINGER DRESSING

½ cup extra virgin olive oil

¼ cup balsamic vinegar

2 tablespoons soy sauce

2 garlic cloves, minced

2 tablespoons raw honey

2 tablespoons freshly grated ginger

1 teaspoon toasted sesame oil

FRIED PORK

1 tablespoon hot sauce

2 tablespoons light or dark brown sugar

1 garlic clove, minced

¼ teaspoon kosher salt

12 ounces pork tenderloin, trimmed and sliced crosswise into ½-inch thick slices

Canola oil cooking spray

3 cups baby spinach leaves

1 cup roughly chopped bell peppers (red, yellow, and orange)

¼ cup chopped fresh chives

TO MAKE THE SESAME-GINGER DRESSING:

① Place all the dressing ingredients in a food processor and process until smooth, about 1 minute. Cover and set aside.

TO MAKE THE FRIED PORK:

① In a large bowl, combine the hot sauce, brown sugar, garlic, and salt and mix well to thoroughly combine. Add the pork slices and toss to coat. Let marinate at room temperature for at least 1 hour.

② Remove the pork from the marinade, shaking off any excess, and place in the basket. Spray on all sides with canola oil. Air fry at 400° F until cooked through, about 10 minutes, flipping halfway through cooking time.

③ Toss spinach with peppers and chives. Top with Fried Pork and Sesame-Ginger Dressing.

◯ Makes 4 servings

COUNTRY FRIED PORK CHOPS

Spiking the breadcrumbs with garlic powder in this recipe punches up the flavor of regular breaded pork chops.

4 pork loin chops

1 teaspoon kosher salt

1 teaspoon freshly ground black pepper

1 cup Italian-seasoned Breadcrumbs (page 143)

1 tablespoon garlic powder

1 cup flour

1 large egg, beaten

Olive oil cooking spray

① Rinse the pork chops and pat dry with paper towels. Sprinkle with the salt and pepper.

② In a shallow bowl, combine the breadcrumbs and garlic powder. Dip each pork chop into the flour, then the beaten egg, then dredge in the breadcrumb mixture, turning to coat evenly.

③ Spray on all sides with olive oil and place in the basket.

④ Air fry in batches at 400° F for 10 minutes, then flip chops and continue to air fry until cooked through and golden, about 5 minutes.

◯ Makes 4 servings

DIJON-GARLIC PORK TENDERLOIN

I'm absolutely in love with the combination of honey, Dijon mustard, and garlic in the marinade-turned-sauce in this dish. Pork tenderloin is a great way to shake up your family's usual dinner menu without having to do anything extravagant.

1 pound pork tenderloin, sliced into 1-inch-thick rounds

2 teaspoons kosher salt

1½ teaspoons freshly ground black pepper

2 tablespoons honey

2 tablespoons Dijon mustard

4 tablespoons water

2 teaspoons ground ginger

3 garlic cloves, crushed

Pinch of cayenne pepper

1 cup Basic Homemade Breadcrumbs (page 142)

① Sprinkle both sides of the pork rounds with the salt and pepper.

② In a shallow bowl, combine the honey, mustard, water, ginger, garlic, and cayenne pepper and mix well.

③ Dip each pork round into the honey-Dijon mixture, then press each side into the breadcrumbs, coating evenly.

④ Place the rounds in the basket of the air fryer, leaving space between each one.

⑤ Air fry at 400° F for 10 minutes, then flip and air fry until golden brown, about 5 more minutes.

◯ Makes 4 servings

SMOKEHOUSE RIBS WITH HOMEMADE BBQ SAUCE

I'm a huge ribs fan, and making them in the air fryer is a lot easier and faster than in a traditional smoker. My smoky rub and homemade sauce make this recipe rival the ribs at any blue-ribbon BBQ joint.

RUB

1 tablespoon chili powder

1 tablespoon cumin

1 teaspoon garlic powder

1 teaspoon ground mustard

2 tablespoons kosher salt

1 teaspoon freshly ground black pepper

1 tablespoon dark brown sugar

RIBS

1 rack baby back ribs

½ cup red wine vinegar

SAUCE

3 tablespoons tomato sauce

2 tablespoons balsamic vinegar

2 tablespoons dark brown sugar

1 tablespoon mustard

1 tablespoon garlic powder

1 tablespoon sea salt

TO MAKE THE RUB:

① In a large bowl, combine all of the Rub ingredients and mix well. Set aside.

TO MAKE THE RIBS:

① Rinse the rack and pat dry. With a sharp knife, slice the rack into ribs.

② Pour the red wine vinegar into a bowl. Toss the ribs in the vinegar, then add the ribs to the bowl containing the Rub. Rub the spice mixture into the meat with your fingers.

③ Stand the ribs up in the basket and air fry at 360° F for 30 minutes.

TO MAKE THE SAUCE:

① Meanwhile, in a small saucepan, combine all of the sauce ingredients and heat over medium-low heat, stirring continuously, until the sugar dissolves, 3–5 minutes.

② Remove the ribs from the air fryer. Brush sauce onto cooked ribs and return ribs to air fryer for 5 minutes, or until sauce is bubbly and ribs are tender.

◯ Makes 2 servings

SPICY FRIED MEATBALLS

Meatballs are a true crowd-pleaser, whether served on top of spaghetti, with a side of rice, or speared with toothpicks for a simply delicious appetizer. Who doesn't love a giant bite of meaty goodness? Especially when it has the perfect crunchy shell and moist inside that the air fryer provides.

- **1 pound ground chuck**
- **1 small onion, finely chopped**
- **1 garlic clove, minced**
- **1 large egg, beaten**
- **¼ cup Panko Breadcrumbs (page 142)**
- **1 teaspoon grated ginger**
- **½ teaspoon ground cumin**
- **½ teaspoon chili powder**
- **1 teaspoon salt**
- **¼ teaspoon freshly ground black pepper**
- **Olive oil**

① In a large bowl, loosely mix all of the ingredients except the olive oil together with your hands.

② Scoop approximately 3 tablespoons of the mixture into the palm of your hand and roll into a ball. Repeat with the remaining mixture.

③ Brush the meatballs on all sides with olive oil and place them in the basket, leaving room between each one.

④ Air fry in batches at 400° F until cooked through and golden, about 12 minutes. Shake the basket once or twice during cooking time to flip the meatballs.

◯ Makes 4–5 servings

BAD-A** SKIRT STEAK

You may consider yourself a grill person through and through, but once you try steak that's been made in the air fryer you might change your mind forever. Skirt steak is full of flavor but is one of the tougher cuts of meat, so for the best results, marinate it overnight to allow the vinegar and soy sauce to tenderize it.

½ cup soy sauce

2 tablespoons extra virgin olive oil

½ cup light brown sugar

¼ teaspoon ground ginger

¼ teaspoon black pepper

1 garlic clove, minced

1 pound skirt steak, sliced into 4 sections

① In a medium bowl, combine all of the ingredients except for the steak.

② Place the steak in a resealable plastic bag and pour the marinade over it, ensuring that all of the meat is covered. Press the air out of the bag before sealing, then wrap it tightly around the steak. Refrigerate for at least 2 hours, but preferably overnight.

③ Remove the meat from the refrigerator and let sit at room temperature for at least 30 minutes before cooking. Remove steak from the marinade and pat dry with paper towels.

④ Place 2 of the steak cuts in the basket. Air fry at 390° F for 10–12 minutes, depending on desired level of doneness. Repeat with additional steak cuts.

⑤ Let the steak sit for at least 15 minutes after removing it from the air fryer before you serve.

○ Makes 4 servings

SPECTACULAR
SIDES

ROADSIDE DINER ONION RINGS

POTATOES AU GRATIN

ROSEMARY ROASTED RED POTATOES

PERFECT POTATO PANCAKES

STRING BEAN FRIES

FOUR-CHEESE PHYLLO TRIANGLES

FRIED GREEN TOMATOES

SUMMER VEGETABLE GRATIN

ROADSIDE DINER ONION RINGS

My favorite thing about any road trip, of course, is the food you find along the way. These onion rings are reminiscent of the crunchy, almost sweet perfection you can find at a country roadside diner that has a fry cook who knows every trick. Make sure to use a Vidalia onion to hit all the right notes.

1 small Vidalia onion, peeled and sliced into rounds ⅛-inch thick

1 cup self-rising flour

1 teaspoon kosher salt, plus additional for sprinkling

½ teaspoon freshly ground black pepper

2 large eggs, beaten

1 cup Panko Breadcrumbs (page 142)

Canola oil cooking spray

① Soak the onion slices in ice water for 30 minutes to firm them up and seal in flavor. Drain in a colander.

② In a large bowl, combine the flour, salt, and pepper and toss gently to combine. Dredge each of the onion rings in the flour mixture, then dip into the beaten egg, then coat evenly with the breadcrumbs. Shake off any excess coating and spray with canola oil.

③ Place the onion rings in the air fryer basket, making sure to leave room between each one. Air fry in batches at 400° F until golden, about 7 minutes. Sprinkle with salt to taste.

○ Makes 4 servings

POTATOES AU GRATIN

Potatoes au gratin translates into "potatoes with cheese," and you might know them as "scalloped potatoes." However, I prefer the French name as they got their start as a French comfort food. Make them with Gruyère to keep the experience authentic.

½ cup whole milk

½ cup cream

½ cup Parmesan cheese

1 garlic clove, diced

½ teaspoon freshly grated nutmeg

½ teaspoon kosher salt

1 teaspoon freshly ground black pepper

3 medium russet potatoes, peeled and thinly sliced (⅛-inch thick or thinner)

Canola oil cooking spray

½ cup grated Gruyère cheese

① In a large bowl, whisk together the milk, cream, Parmesan, garlic, nutmeg, salt, and pepper. Add the potato slices and mix well to coat.

② Spray the bottom of the air fryer pan with canola oil. Then pour the potato mixture into the pan.

③ Air fry at 390° F for 10 minutes, then top with the Gruyère. Continue frying until cheese is bubbly and begins to brown, about 5 minutes.

◯ Makes 4–6 servings

ROSEMARY ROASTED RED POTATOES

Roasted potatoes are insanely easy to prepare, especially in an air fryer, yet they'll still get you accolades from friends and family every time. I like to use both dried and fresh rosemary in my version to give the potatoes more depth of flavor.

2 pounds small red potatoes

1 tablespoon extra virgin olive oil

1 teaspoon kosher salt

½ teaspoon freshly ground black pepper

1 teaspoon dried rosemary

1 tablespoon chopped fresh rosemary

① Halve or quarter the potatoes, depending on their size. You want each piece to be bite-sized.

② In a large bowl, toss the potato pieces with olive oil, salt, pepper, and dried rosemary until thoroughly coated.

③ Air fry the potatoes in batches, placing them in a single layer in the cooking basket. Start out at 360° F for 10 minutes. Then shake the basket to flip the potatoes and air fry at 400° F until potatoes are cooked through, about 10–15 minutes more. Top with the fresh rosemary.

◯ Makes 4–6 servings

PERFECT POTATO PANCAKES

Potato pancakes, or latkes, have been around about as long as Europe has, with cultural variations popping up in places as diverse as Poland, England, and Sweden. Many Jewish families also make them to celebrate Hanukkah. If you've never had one, you're in for a treat. They're crunchy on the outside and moist on the inside, so naturally they're a perfect fit for air frying.

2 medium or large russet potatoes, peeled

1 small onion

1 large egg, beaten

1 teaspoon kosher salt

½ teaspoon freshly ground pepper

3 tablespoons all-purpose flour

① Put the potatoes in a pot and cover with water. Bring to a boil, and cook potatoes until you can just sink a fork into them—they should still be firm—about 10 minutes. Drain and let them cool enough to handle. Using a box grater, grate the onion and potatoes and toss together to combine. Place the grated mixture in a tight mesh strainer and press to release excess liquid. Blot the mixture with a paper towel and place in a large bowl.

② Add the egg, salt, and pepper and stir with a fork to mix. Next, add the flour 1 tablespoon at a time, mixing thoroughly between each addition.

③ Scoop about ¼ of the mixture into the palm of your hand and form it into a patty. Repeat with remaining mixture. Place 1 patty at a time in the air fryer basket.

④ Air fry in batches at 400° F until golden brown, about 20 minutes.

◯ Makes 4 servings

STRING BEAN FRIES

These string bean fries are a great way to get your kids to eat their veggies, especially if you prepare them with one of my sauces or condiments (pages 129–140). Make sure to refrigerate them for a bit before air frying them, which helps the breading stick.

½ pound fresh string (green) beans, trimmed

1 large egg

¼ cup 2% or whole milk

1 cup Italian-seasoned Breadcrumbs (page 143)

½ teaspoon chili powder

½ teaspoon garlic powder

½ teaspoon onion powder

½ cup all-purpose flour

① Blanch the string beans by heating them in boiling water for 2–3 minutes, then immediately rinsing with cold water to stop the cooking process. Drain, then pat dry with paper towels and refrigerate for 30 minutes.

② In a shallow bowl, whisk together the egg and the milk.

③ In a separate shallow bowl, combine the breadcrumbs, chili powder, garlic powder, and onion powder and mix well.

④ Dredge each string bean in the flour, then dip into the beaten egg, then coat evenly with the breadcrumb mixture. Place the beans in the air fryer basket, leaving space between each one.

⑤ Air fry in batches at 400° F until golden brown, about 10 minutes.

○ Makes 4 servings

FOUR-CHEESE PHYLLO TRIANGLES

Cheese, cheese, and more cheese, all wrapped in a delicate pastry dough. What's not to love about that? This decadent Mediterranean specialty combines four of my favorite cheeses: feta, Parmesan, Gruyère, and ricotta.

2 cups crumbled feta cheese

1⅓ cups freshly grated Parmesan cheese

1 cup shredded Gruyère cheese

½ cup ricotta cheese

¾ cup heavy cream

½ teaspoon freshly ground black pepper

8 (14 x 18 inch) sheets of frozen phyllo (filo) dough, thawed

¼ cup extra virgin olive oil, divided

2 large eggs, beaten

① In a large bowl, mix together the cheeses, cream, and pepper. Cover and refrigerate for 30 minutes.

② Spread out 4 of the phyllo dough sheets on a clean work surface and brush the tops with oil. Top each of these sheets with an additional sheet, and brush these tops with oil as well. Taking both sheets, fold the dough in half lengthwise so you have a long sheet with one of the short ends closest to you.

③ With the tip of your finger or a brush, apply a small amount of the beaten egg to all the edges of one of the dough sheets, like a frame.

④ Spoon about 2 heaping tablespoons of the cheese mixture onto the dough, at the top right, just under where you brushed the egg. Then fold the top left corner of the dough diagonally over it, creating a triangle with the filling underneath. Press the edges to seal the dough.

⑤ Carefully fold this filled triangle straight down, then diagonally down to the left, then straight down, then diagonally down to the right, repeating until you have used the rest of the dough sheet. Repeat steps 3 through 5 with remaining dough sheets.

⑥ Brush the outside of the filled triangles with the remaining olive oil. Place them in the basket, leaving space between each one.

⑦ Air fry in batches (if necessary) at 360° F until golden brown, about 15 minutes. Let the triangles cool for about 20 minutes before serving to allow the cheese to set.

◯ Makes 2–4 servings

FRIED GREEN TOMATOES

This quintessential Southern classic comes out perfectly when air fried: crispy on the outside, juicy on the inside. Make sure to eat them while they're hot.

3 large green tomatoes
2 large eggs
¼ cup buttermilk
¾ cup all-purpose flour
1½ cups Panko Breadcrumbs (page 142)
Olive oil cooking spray
Kosher salt and freshly ground black pepper, to taste

① Cut the tomatoes into ¼-inch-thick slices and place on paper towels to absorb excess liquid.

② Whisk together the eggs and buttermilk.

③ Dredge a tomato slice in the flour on each side, then dip into the egg mixture, then press each side gently into the breadcrumbs, coating evenly. Spray both sides with olive oil. Repeat with remaining tomato slices. Sprinkle with salt and pepper.

④ Place tomato slices on a rack in the basket, making sure to leave space between each one. Air fry in batches at 400° F until golden, about 5 minutes.

◯ Makes 4–6 servings

SUMMER VEGETABLE GRATIN

This delicious dish, which utilizes seasonal veggies, is substantial enough to hold its own as a main dish on hot summer nights.

1 medium zucchini

1 medium yellow squash

1 small eggplant, peeled

1 tablespoon salt

2 tablespoons olive oil

½ cup shredded Cheddar cheese

½ cup Italian-seasoned Breadcrumbs (page 143)

1 garlic clove, minced

½ teaspoon freshly ground black pepper

¼ cup freshly grated Parmesan cheese

Olive oil cooking spray

2 tablespoons chopped fresh Italian flat-leaf parsley

① With a box grater, grate the zucchini, yellow squash, and eggplant. Toss with the salt and let sit in a colander to sweat out moisture for at least 30 minutes and up to 90 minutes. Rinse with cool water to get rid of excess salt, then pat dry with paper towels. Toss with the olive oil and Cheddar cheese.

② In a small bowl, combine the breadcrumbs, garlic, pepper, and Parmesan cheese and toss to combine.

③ Spray the air fryer pan with olive oil, then add the vegetable mixture. Top with breadcrumb mixture.

④ Air fry at 350° F until vegetables are tender, about 25 minutes. Top with parsley.

○ Makes 4 servings

CHIPS
AND
FRIES

APPLE PIE CHIPS

PLANTAIN CHIPS

SWEET 'N' SPICY SWEET-POTATO CHIPS

HERBED POTATO CHIPS

CRUNCHY KALE CHIPS

EGGPLANT PARMESAN CHIPS

SPICY YUCCA CHIPS

ZUCCHINI-PARMESAN CHIPS

BETTER-THAN-FAST-FOOD FRIES

STEAKHOUSE FRIES

SPICED SWEET-POTATO FRIES

APPLE PIE CHIPS

Apple Pie Chips are a great way to satisfy that midafternoon sweet tooth. Leave the peels on to give the chips a nice texture—not to mention added vitamins and nutrients.

2 Gala apples

2 tablespoons unsalted butter, melted

1 teaspoon ground cinnamon

2 teaspoons light brown sugar

① Core the apples and slice them into thin discs using a mandoline slicer or as thinly as possible with a knife.

② Lay the apple slices on a clean work surface and drizzle with the melted butter, then sprinkle with the cinnamon and brown sugar.

③ Place the apple slices in the basket of the air fryer, making sure they don't overlap.

④ Air fry in batches at 360° F until crispy, about 25 minutes. Shake the basket to flip the chips 1 or 2 times during cooking time.

○ Makes 2–4 servings

PLANTAIN CHIPS

A cousin of the banana, plantains make perfect chips because they have almost as much starch as potatoes. Meanwhile, their almost sweet taste makes them phenomenal when paired with salsa, black bean dip, or guacamole.

2 green plantains

1 tablespoon extra virgin olive oil

Kosher salt and freshly ground black pepper, to taste

① Peel and slice the plantains into thin discs using a mandoline slicer or as thinly as possible with a knife. Brush each slice with the olive oil on both sides.

② Place the plantain slices in the basket of the air fryer, making sure they don't overlap.

③ Air fry in batches at 360° F until crispy, about 25 minutes. Sprinkle with salt and pepper to taste.

◯ Makes 3–4 servings

SWEET 'N' SPICY SWEET-POTATO CHIPS

Make extra, because these spiced sweet-potato chips are going to go fast. The combination of salty and sweet makes them irresistible alone or with yogurt-based dips (pages 134–135) and hummus.

2 large sweet potatoes, peeled

1 tablespoon olive oil

1 tablespoon smoked paprika

1 tablespoon garlic powder

½ tablespoon light brown sugar

½ tablespoon onion powder

½ teaspoon chili powder

1 teaspoon kosher salt

1 teaspoon freshly ground black pepper

① Slice the sweet potatoes into thin discs using a mandoline slicer or as thinly as possible with a knife.

② In a large bowl, toss the sweet-potato slices with the olive oil to thoroughly coat. Add the remaining ingredients and toss to coat.

③ Place the potato slices in the basket of the air fryer, making sure they don't overlap. Air fry in batches at 390° F until crispy, about 12 minutes.

○ Makes 4–5 servings

HERBED POTATO CHIPS

So much better than any bagged chips, these thin and crispy treats are seasoned with herbs for flavor instead of excess salt.

2 medium russet potatoes

1 tablespoon extra virgin olive oil

1 teaspoon dried rosemary

1 teaspoon dried thyme

1 teaspoon dried oregano

1 teaspoon kosher salt

① Slice the potatoes into thin discs using a mandoline slicer or as thinly as possible with a knife.

② Place the potato slices into a bowl of ice water and soak for 30 minutes. Drain in a colander, then pat dry with paper towels.

③ In a large bowl, toss the potato slices with the olive oil. Place the potatoes in the basket of the air fryer, making sure they don't overlap.

④ Air fry in batches at 330° F until crispy, about 30 minutes.

⑤ While chips are still warm, toss with the remaining ingredients and serve.

◯ Makes 2–4 servings

CRUNCHY KALE CHIPS

Kale has been hailed as a "superfood," thanks to all its amazing health benefits, and one of my favorite ways to eat it is simply crisped up in the air fryer. I call these "chips" even though they're actually crispy-yet-delicate leaves of kale.

1 bunch kale

1½ tablespoons extra virgin olive oil

Sea salt, to taste

① Remove the stems from the kale leaves and cut the leaves into squares of 1–2 inches. Make sure they're completely dry by patting them with paper towels.

② Drizzle the kale with the olive oil and sprinkle with salt.

③ Place kale leaves in the basket of the air fryer, being careful not to let them overlap. Air fry in batches at 360° F until edges are curled and crispy but not burned, about 15 minutes.

④ Let cool before serving.

○ Makes 4 servings

EGGPLANT PARMESAN CHIPS

Stop whatever you're doing and go make these right now: You've never tasted anything like Eggplant Parmesan Chips. Meaty, crunchy, cheesy, yet they're healthy for you! Give them to your kids, give them to your spouse, give them to the whole neighborhood! That is, if you don't want to just hoard them for yourself.

1 large eggplant, peeled

2 teaspoons kosher salt

1 large egg, beaten

2 tablespoons whole milk

2 cups Panko Breadcrumbs (page 142)

½ cup freshly grated Parmesan cheese

Olive oil cooking spray

① Slice the eggplant lengthwise into quarters, then slice each section widthwise as thinly as possible to make the chips. Toss the chips with the salt and let sit in a colander to drain for 30 minutes. Rinse the chips in cool water to remove excess salt and lay on paper towels to dry. Once dry, place on a cookie sheet and freeze for 1 hour.

② In a shallow bowl, whisk together the egg and milk.

③ In a separate shallow bowl, mix together the breadcrumbs and Parmesan cheese.

④ Remove the eggplant chips from the freezer. Dip each one into the egg mixture, then dredge each side in the breadcrumb mixture, coating well. Shake off any excess breadcrumbs.

⑤ Place the chips in the basket, making sure they don't overlap. Spray all sides with olive oil.

⑥ Air fry in batches at 400° F until crispy, about 5 minutes.

◯ Makes approximately 2 servings

SPICY YUCCA CHIPS

Yucca is probably one of those foods that's been sitting in your produce section all along, and you just didn't know it. A root that's used in a lot of South American dishes, it's full of flavor and makes unforgettable chips.

2 yucca roots
¾ teaspoon kosher salt
1 tablespoon chili powder
Pinch of cayenne pepper

① Slice the yucca into thin discs using a mandoline or as thinly as possible with a knife. Lay them in a single layer on paper towels and sprinkle with the remaining ingredients. Let sit for 15 minutes.

② Place the slices in the basket of the air fryer, making sure they don't overlap. Air fry in batches at 360° F until crispy, about 25 minutes. Shake the basket to flip the chips 1 or 2 times during cooking time.

◯ Makes 4 servings

ZUCCHINI-PARMESAN CHIPS

This is a different take on my Zucchini Fritters (page 29). In this version, the zucchini is sliced thin for even more crunch.

2 medium zucchini

1 tablespoon salt

½ cup Italian-seasoned Breadcrumbs (page 143)

½ cup freshly grated Parmesan cheese

1 large egg, beaten

Canola oil cooking spray

Kosher salt and freshly ground black pepper, to taste

① Slice the zucchini into thin discs using a mandoline slicer or as thinly as possible with a knife. Toss the zucchini slices with the salt and let drain in a colander for 30 minutes. Rinse thoroughly with cold water to get rid of excess salt. Then lay the zucchini slices on paper towels and pat dry.

② In a shallow bowl, combine the breadcrumbs and Parmesan cheese.

③ Dip the zucchini slices in the egg, then dredge on each side in the breadcrumbs to coat thoroughly. Spray on each side with canola oil.

④ Place the slices in the basket of the air fryer, making sure they don't overlap. Air fry in batches at 390° F until crispy, about 10 minutes. Sprinkle with salt and pepper to taste.

◯ Makes 2 servings

BETTER-THAN-FAST-FOOD FRIES

The secret to the crispiest French fries, whether in a traditional fryer or an air fryer, is frying them twice. After eating these fries, you'll never get a craving for the fast-food version again—because these are better.

2 medium russet potatoes, peeled and sliced into ¼-inch thick strips
1 tablespoon peanut or canola oil
1 teaspoon sea salt

① Soak the potato strips in ice water for 1 hour to remove the starch. Drain in a colander.

② Place the strips in the air fryer basket, making sure to leave space between each one, and air fry in batches at 400° F for 15 minutes. Then remove from the air fryer and let cool at room temperature for 10 minutes.

③ Toss the strips with the oil and salt.

④ Place the strips back in the basket and continue to air fry in batches at 400° F until golden brown, about 15 more minutes.

○ Makes 3–4 servings

STEAKHOUSE FRIES

These beefed-up fries are just like the ones you'd get in a steakhouse, but without all the fat. Do yourself a favor and don't peel these potatoes. Not only are potato skins rich in nutrients, they give these fries a rustic taste that sets them apart from average fries.

4 medium russet potatoes, sliced into ¼-inch thick strips

3 tablespoons extra virgin olive oil

1 teaspoon sweet or smoked paprika

¼ teaspoon kosher salt

¼ teaspoon freshly ground black pepper

½ teaspoon chopped fresh Italian flat-leaf parsley

① Soak the potato strips in ice water for 1 hour to remove the starch. Drain in a colander.

② Place the strips in the air fryer basket, making sure to leave space between each one, and air fry in batches at 400° F for 15 minutes. Then remove from the air fryer and let cool at room temperature for 10 minutes.

③ Toss the strips with the olive oil, paprika, salt, and pepper.

④ Place the strips back in the basket and continue to air fry in batches at 400° F until golden brown, about 15 more minutes. Top with the parsley.

◯ Makes 4–6 servings

SPICED SWEET-POTATO FRIES

While some people are French fry purists, others can't get enough of the taste of sweet-potato fries. Luckily, we can all live in harmony by making a plate of each. This sweet-potato fries recipe includes a pinch of cayenne for a kick.

2 large sweet potatoes, peeled and sliced into ¼-inch thick strips

1 tablespoon extra virgin olive oil

1 teaspoon ground cumin

Pinch of cayenne pepper

½ teaspoon kosher salt

① Soak the sweet-potato strips in ice water for 1 hour to remove the starch. Drain in a colander.

② Place the strips in the air fryer basket, making sure to leave space between each one, and air fry in batches at 400° F for 15 minutes. Then remove from the air fryer and let cool at room temperature for 10 minutes.

③ Toss the strips with the olive oil, cumin, cayenne pepper, and salt.

④ Place back in the basket and continue to air fry in batches at 400° F until golden brown, about 15 more minutes.

○ Makes 3–4 servings

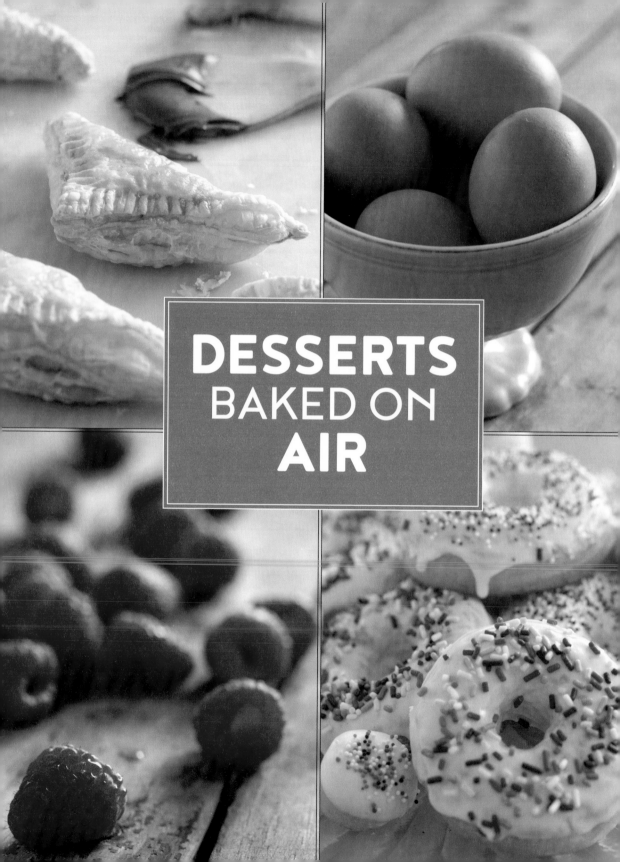

DESSERTS
BAKED ON
AIR

PUFFY GLAZED DOUGHNUTS

LIGHT 'N' AIRY BLUEBERRY MUFFINS

CHOCOLATE VELVET CAKE

FRIED "EVERYTHING" BROWNIES

APPLE TARTLETS

BERRY CHEESECAKE PUFFS

FRIED RASPBERRY PIES

BERRY CRUMBLE

CHOCOLATE-PEANUT BUTTER POCKETS

PUFFY GLAZED DOUGHNUTS

DOUGHNUTS. They're a national obsession for good reason—nothing tops them for decadent sweetness. Unfortunately, they're not great for you, unless you make them in your air fryer. If you prefer an even easier recipe, you can substitute refrigerated biscuit dough for homemade and a tub of frosting for the glaze—it doesn't get easier than that.

DOUGHNUTS

1¼ cups milk, warmed

¼ cup granulated sugar

1 (.25 ounce) packet active dry yeast

2 large eggs, beaten

1 stick unsalted butter, melted

1 teaspoon salt

4¼ cups all-purpose flour, plus more if needed

Canola oil cooking spray

GLAZE

1½ cups powdered sugar

2 tablespoons whole milk

2 teaspoons pure vanilla extract

TO MAKE THE DOUGHNUTS:

① In a medium bowl, combine the warm milk and sugar; mix until the sugar dissolves. Then add the yeast and let sit until the mixture starts to bubble, 5–10 minutes.

② In a separate medium bowl, whisk together the eggs and the melted butter.

③ In the bowl of an electric stand mixer fitted with a dough hook attachment, combine the egg-butter mixture, the milk mixture, and the salt. Mix on low speed until well combined, about 1 minute.

④ While continuing to mix on low speed, add the flour 1 cup at a time to the mixer bowl, allowing each cup to be absorbed before adding the next cup.

⑤ Continue mixing until the dough begins to pull away from the sides of the bowl, about 5 minutes after the flour is fully combined. If the dough is too wet, add more flour 1 tablespoon at a time.

⑥ Place the dough in a lightly greased bowl, then cover and refrigerate overnight (at least 8 hours).

⑦ Remove from the refrigerator and place in a warm location to rise for 2 hours.

⑧ Turn out the dough onto a floured work surface and roll with a rolling pin until it is about ¼-inch thick. Cut into 1-inch rounds with a biscuit cutter, cookie cutter, or pint glass, then cut a hole in the center of each with a smaller cookie cutter or shot glass.

⑨ Place each doughnut on a parchment-lined baking sheet. Cover with clean kitchen towels and return to warm location to let rise another 2 hours.

⑩ Place the doughnuts in the basket of the air fryer, making sure to leave space between each one. Spray on both sides with canola oil.

⑪ Air fry in batches at 400° F until golden, about 5 minutes, flipping halfway through cooking time. As soon as the doughnuts are cool enough to touch, dip each in the glaze.

○ Makes 10–12 doughnuts

TO MAKE THE GLAZE:

① Combine all of the glaze ingredients in a bowl and stir until smooth.

LIGHT 'N' AIRY BLUEBERRY MUFFINS

Believe it or not, air fryers are even great for making muffins—just double up on muffin cups to keep the muffins intact since you aren't using a muffin tin. These sweet breakfast treats can be whipped up super fast in the air fryer, so get ready to serve freshly baked muffins every morning!

⅔ cup all-purpose flour

1½ teaspoons baking powder

3 tablespoons granulated sugar

Pinch of salt

1 large egg

½ teaspoon vanilla

⅓ cup 2% or whole milk

3 tablespoons unsalted butter, melted

½ cup fresh blueberries

① In a large bowl, mix together the flour, baking powder, sugar, and salt.

② In a medium bowl, whisk together the egg, vanilla, and milk, then add the melted butter and stir well to combine.

③ Add the wet mixture to the flour mixture and whisk just until lumps disappear. Gently fold in the blueberries.

④ Place 4 doubled-up muffin cups into the air fryer basket and carefully spoon the batter into the cups, filling ¾ of the way full.

⑤ Air fry at 320° F until a toothpick inserted into the center of a muffin comes out clean, about 15–20 minutes.

◯ Makes 4 muffins

CHOCOLATE VELVET CAKE

Mug cakes are yummy little cakes made in coffee mugs that you don't have to share with a single soul. This is my take. You can enjoy the cake on its own, or top with frosting or whipped cream and berries. Share if you must, but I recommend eating the whole thing yourself!

1½ cups all-purpose flour

¾ cup granulated sugar

3 tablespoons unsweetened cocoa powder

1 teaspoon baking soda

½ teaspoon kosher salt

1 teaspoon pure vanilla extract

¼ cup canola oil

1 cup water

1 tablespoon white vinegar

Canola oil cooking spray

① In a large bowl, combine all of the ingredients except the cooking spray with an electric hand mixer until just blended.

② Spray the air fryer's pan with the cooking spray and pour the cake mixture into the pan.

③ Air fry at 330° F until a toothpick inserted into the middle of the cake comes out clean, about 30 minutes.

④ Remove the cake from the air fryer and let sit another 30 minutes to cool.

○ Makes 1–2 servings

FRIED "EVERYTHING" BROWNIES

If you love chocolate as much as I do, you'll go nuts for these fried brownies that have a little bit of everything—semi-sweet chocolate, white chocolate, and macadamia nuts.

> **1 large egg**
>
> **⅓ cup granulated sugar**
>
> **1 teaspoon pure vanilla extract**
>
> **⅓ cup semi-sweet chocolate chips**
>
> **1 tablespoon salted butter**
>
> **⅓ cup self-rising flour**
>
> **2 tablespoons white chocolate chips**
>
> **2 tablespoons chopped macadamia nuts**
>
> **Canola oil cooking spray**

① In a large mixing bowl, whisk the egg. While continuing to whisk, add the sugar. When fully incorporated, add the vanilla extract and continue to whisk until well combined. Set aside.

② In a small saucepan over medium-low heat, melt the semi-sweet chocolate chips with the butter, stirring constantly but gently.

③ When fully melted and combined, pour over the sugar mixture and fold in to combine thoroughly. Then stir in the flour. Finally, add the white chocolate chips and macadamia nuts and stir until well combined.

④ Spray the air fryer pan with canola oil and pour the mixture into the pan.

⑤ Air fry at 360° F until the top of the brownies is firm, about 20 minutes. Let cool for at least 30 minutes before slicing into sections and serving.

○ Makes 4–6 servings

APPLE TARTLETS

An apple tart can be a bit of a production, but these are so easy you can even have the kids help you make them.

   3 small baking apples such as Gala, Granny Smith, or Golden Delicious

   2 teaspoons raw honey

   ⅛ teaspoon cinnamon

   1 teaspoon lemon zest

   1 teaspoon fresh lemon juice

   1 tablespoon unsalted butter, melted

   1 (10 x 15 inch) sheet frozen or refrigerated puff pastry dough, thawed but still cool

   1 large egg, beaten

① Core and peel the apples and chop into ¼-inch cubes. Set aside.

② In a large bowl, combine the honey, cinnamon, lemon zest, lemon juice, and melted butter and stir well to combine. Add the apple cubes and toss to coat well.

③ With a pizza cutter, slice the puff pastry sheet into 15 squares of roughly the same size—if the longer side is facing you, make 2 equally spaced horizontal cuts and then 4 equally spaced vertical cuts.

④ Spoon a heaping teaspoon of the apple mixture into the center of each square. With the tip of your finger or a brush, apply a small amount of the beaten egg to all the edges of each square, like a frame.

⑤ Form the tartlets into dumpling shapes by pulling up two opposite corners and pinching them together, then pinching together the other corners.

⑥ Place the tartlets in the basket of the air fryer, leaving plenty of room between each one.

⑦ Air fry in batches at 360° F until golden brown, about 20 minutes.

○ Makes 15 tartlets

BERRY CHEESECAKE PUFFS

What I love about puff pastry is how light and fluffy it gets, especially in an air fryer. Pack it with cheesecake and whatever berries are local and in season, and you have an explosion of fresh summer sweetness ready to pop in your mouth.

4 ounces cream cheese

½ cup granulated sugar

2 large eggs, divided

½ teaspoon vanilla

2 tablespoons chopped white chocolate

½ cup chopped strawberries, blueberries, raspberries, and/or blackberries

1 (10 x 15 inch) sheet refrigerated or frozen puff pastry dough, thawed

Canola oil cooking spray

① In a large mixing bowl, combine the cream cheese and sugar. Beat on medium until well blended. Continuing to beat on medium, add 1 of the eggs, then the vanilla. Blend until well mixed, about 1–2 minutes more. Fold in the white chocolate and berries.

② Place the puff pastry on a floured work surface with the longer edge closest to you. Using a pizza cutter, cut it in half horizontally, then make 3 equally spaced cuts vertically to form 8 rectangular-shaped pieces.

③ In a small bowl, beat the remaining egg. With the tip of your finger or a brush, apply a small amount of the egg to all the edges of each rectangle, like a frame.

④ Spoon a scant tablespoon of the cream cheese mixture onto the bottom half of each rectangle just above the egged edge. Fold the top half of the rectangle over the cream cheese mixture to form a square. Press the tines of a fork along all 4 edges of the square and repeat with the remaining dough and filling.

⑤ Place the dough squares in the basket of the air fryer, leaving plenty of room between each one. Spray on all sides with canola oil.

⑥ Air fry at 360° F until golden brown, about 10–15 minutes.

◯ Makes 8 puffs

FRIED RASPBERRY PIES

If you ever lusted after those store-bought raspberry snack pies as a kid, this dessert will hit you in all the right spots, and it's even better than the original.

1 cup chopped raspberries

2 tablespoons granulated sugar

2 teaspoons cornstarch

1 teaspoon lemon juice

¼ teaspoon pure vanilla extract

Pinch of salt

1 (20 ounce) package frozen empanada wrappers, thawed

1 large egg, beaten

Canola oil cooking spray

① In a medium bowl, combine the raspberries, sugar, cornstarch, lemon juice, vanilla extract, and salt.

② Lay out the empanada wrappers on a floured countertop. With the tip of your finger or a brush, apply a small amount of the egg to all the edges of each wrapper.

③ Spread a heaping tablespoon of pie filling over each wrapper, then fold each wrapper in half and press the edges together with the tines of a fork.

④ Place the pies in the air fryer basket, leaving plenty of space between each one. Spray on all sides with canola oil. Air fry in batches at 360° F until golden brown, about 20 minutes. Let cool for 15–20 minutes before serving.

◯ Makes 10–12 pies

BERRY CRUMBLE

This sweet crumble can be made with a variety of different fruits, so have fun and experiment. Try pears and pecans, apples and raisins, peaches and blackberries, or my favorite combo, raspberries and blueberries.

1 cup raspberries

1 cup blueberries

1 teaspoon fresh lemon juice

¼ cup granulated sugar, divided

¼ cup all-purpose flour

½ cup rolled oats

¼ teaspoon pure vanilla extract

¼ cup dark brown sugar

3 tablespoons cold unsalted butter, sliced into chunks

Canola oil cooking spray

① In a large bowl, combine the raspberries, blueberries, lemon juice, and ½ of the granulated sugar. Toss gently to coat the berries.

② In a medium bowl, combine the flour, oats, vanilla extract, brown sugar, and remaining granulated sugar. Then mash the butter into the mixture, piece by piece, until the mixture becomes crumbly.

③ Spray the air fryer pan with canola oil and pour the raspberry-blueberry mixture into the pan. Then sprinkle the butter-flour mixture evenly over the top.

④ Air fry at 390° F until the crumble is golden brown and the fruit is bubbly, about 12 minutes.

◯ Makes 2–4 servings

CHOCOLATE-PEANUT BUTTER POCKETS

Chocolate and peanut butter are a match made in heaven—or a puff pastry pocket. If you love chocolate-hazelnut spread but have trouble not simply eating it out of the container, make these instead.

1 (10 x 15 inch) sheet frozen or refrigerated puff pastry dough, thawed but still cool

3 tablespoons creamy peanut butter

3 tablespoons chocolate-hazelnut spread

1 large egg, beaten

① On a piece of parchment paper or a clean, floured work surface, lay out the puff pastry dough. Using a pizza cutter, slice the dough into 6 equal squares.

② Drawing an imaginary line on the diagonal through each dough square, spread peanut butter on one half and chocolate-hazelnut spread on the other. Fold on the diagonal line to create a triangle. Press the dough together with the tines of a fork to seal.

③ Brush both sides of the triangles with the egg and place them in the air fryer basket, leaving space between each one. Air fry in batches at 360° F until golden brown, about 15 minutes. Let cool before serving.

○ Makes 6 pockets

SAUCES
AND HOMEMADE
INGREDIENTS

ROASTED EGGPLANT MEDITERRANEO

SPICY AIOLI

MARINARA DIPPING SAUCE

BASIC VINAIGRETTE

ALMOND PESTO • GRAS PISTAS

CUCUMBER YOGURT SAUCE • LIME CREMA

BASIC RÉMOULADE

CURRY MAYO DIP

HOMEMADE TARTAR SAUCE

SPICY SWEET-AND-SOUR SAUCE

SPICY KETCHUP • ZESTY MUSTARD SAUCE

T-1 STEAK SAUCE

LEMON BUTTER • A.C.G. BUTTER

ROSEMARY AND GARLIC BUTTER

BASIC HOMEMADE BREADCRUMBS

PANKO BREADCRUMBS

ITALIAN-SEASONED BREADCRUMBS

TOASTED BREADCRUMBS

ROASTED EGGPLANT MEDITERRANEO

1 large eggplant, pricked with the tines of a fork

2 garlic cloves, minced

¼ cup crumbled Bulgarian feta cheese

1 teaspoon chopped fresh oregano leaves

1 teaspoon chopped fresh mint leaves

¼ cup fresh lemon juice

1 beefsteak tomato or 2 plum tomatoes, cored and finely chopped

¼ cup pitted black olives (such as Kalamata, oil-cured, or Gaeta), chopped

½ teaspoon kosher salt

¼ teaspoon freshly ground black pepper

① Preheat the oven to 450° F.

② Place the eggplant on a baking sheet in the oven and roast, turning often, until it is very soft when pricked with a fork, about 45 minutes. When it is cool enough to handle, scoop out the flesh, place in a large mixing bowl, and coarsely mash. Discard the skin.

③ Add the remaining ingredients and stir until just blended.

SPICY AIOLI

2 egg yolks

2 garlic cloves, minced

1 tablespoon chili-garlic (sriracha) sauce

1 tablespoon rice vinegar

¼ teaspoon kosher salt

¼ teaspoon freshly ground black pepper

1 cup canola oil

① In a medium bowl, whisk together all of the ingredients except the canola oil.

② While continuing to whisk, add the canola oil in a slow, steady stream, mixing until well blended and smooth.

MARINARA DIPPING SAUCE

2 garlic cloves, minced

¼ cup extra virgin olive oil

1 (28 ounce) can diced San Marzano tomatoes

¼ teaspoon kosher salt

10 basil leaves, torn

① In a large skillet, cook the garlic in the olive oil over medium-low heat until soft, about 1 minute.

② Stir in the tomatoes and salt and bring to a boil. Reduce heat to low and simmer, uncovered, for 15 minutes. Stir in the basil leaves.

BASIC VINAIGRETTE

1 large shallot

½ cup sherry vinegar

2 tablespoons Dijon mustard

½ teaspoon kosher salt

¼ teaspoon freshly ground black pepper

1½ cups extra virgin olive oil

① Place all the ingredients except the olive oil in a food processor and process until mixed well.

② While continuing to process, pour in the olive oil in a slow, steady stream through the pour spout until all of the oil has been fully incorporated.

◄ ALMOND PESTO

¼ cup toasted almonds

2 garlic cloves

2 cups fresh basil leaves

6 tablespoons extra virgin olive oil

½ teaspoon kosher salt

1 teaspoon freshly grated Parmesan cheese

① Place the almonds and garlic cloves in a food processor fitted with a steel blade and pulse until they are well chopped. Add the basil and pulse until combined. While the machine is running, gradually add the oil and process until smooth. Add the salt and Parmesan cheese and process until combined.

② Use immediately or cover and refrigerate up to 2 days.

GRAS PISTAS

5 garlic cloves

1 cup walnuts or pine nuts

1½ cups chopped fresh basil

1 cup chopped fresh Italian flat-leaf parsley

¼ cup chopped fresh mint leaves

½ cup extra virgin olive oil

① Coarsely chop the garlic in a food processor. Add the nuts and continue to pulse. Then add the basil, parsley, and mint and process until well mixed.

② While continuing to process, pour in the olive oil in a slow, steady stream through the pour spout until all of the oil has been fully incorporated.

③ Use immediately or cover and refrigerate up to 1 day.

CUCUMBER YOGURT SAUCE ➔

⅔ English cucumber, peeled, seeded, and chopped

½ cup plain yogurt

¼ cup chopped fresh Italian flat-leaf parsley

¼ cup chopped fresh cilantro leaves

1 jalapeño pepper, seeded and membranes removed

1 garlic clove, minced

⅓ teaspoon kosher salt

¼ teaspoon freshly ground black pepper

① Place all the ingredients in a food processor and process until smooth. Chill for 30 minutes before serving.

LIME CREMA

1 cup plain yogurt

2 teaspoons lime zest

2 teaspoons lime juice

Kosher salt and freshly ground black pepper, to taste

① In a small bowl, combine the first 3 ingredients until well blended. Season with salt and pepper to taste.

BASIC RÉMOULADE

1 tablespoon mayonnaise

1 teaspoon spicy brown mustard

1 teaspoon ketchup

① In a small bowl, combine all the ingredients until well blended.

CURRY MAYO DIP

¼ cup mayonnaise

¼ cup plain yogurt

1 teaspoon curry powder

½ teaspoon garlic powder

Kosher salt and freshly ground black pepper, to taste

① In a small bowl, combine the first 4 ingredients until well blended. Season with salt and pepper to taste.

② Chill for 30 minutes before serving.

HOMEMADE TARTAR SAUCE

½ cup mayonnaise

3 tablespoons capers

2 teaspoons minced red onion

2 teaspoons chopped fresh cilantro

2 teaspoons fresh lemon juice

① In a small bowl, combine all the ingredients until well blended. Chill for 30 minutes before serving.

←SPICY SWEET-AND-SOUR SAUCE

¼ cup orange marmalade

2 tablespoons Thai chili sauce

2 teaspoons fresh lemon juice

① In a small bowl, combine all the ingredients until well blended.

SPICY KETCHUP

1 tablespoon unsalted butter

2 medium white onions, finely chopped

1 (14.5 ounce) can chopped tomatoes

½ cup light brown sugar

½ cup white vinegar

1 teaspoon ground allspice

① In a large skillet, melt the butter over medium heat. Add the onions and cook, stirring occasionally, until caramelized, about 23 minutes.

② Add the tomatoes, brown sugar, vinegar, and allspice. Reduce heat to medium-low and cook, stirring occasionally, until reduced by half, about 30 minutes.

③ Remove from heat and let cool. Pour into a blender and process until smooth. Chill for 30–60 minutes before serving.

ZESTY MUSTARD SAUCE

½ cup mayonnaise

2 tablespoons spicy brown mustard

1 teaspoon fresh lime juice

½ teaspoon Worcestershire sauce

① In a small bowl, combine all the ingredients until well blended.

② Chill for 30 minutes before serving.

T-1 STEAK SAUCE

2 tablespoons olive oil

6 anchovy fillets, drained

3 garlic cloves, minced

2 tablespoons capers, drained

½ cup orange juice

½ cup prune juice

2 tablespoons Dijon mustard

2 tablespoons tomato paste

① Heat the oil in a medium saucepan, then add the anchovies and garlic and cook over medium-low heat, stirring often, about 4 minutes or until garlic is lightly browned. Smash the anchovies with your spoon as they cook.

② Add the capers and cook 1 minute longer.

③ Add the remaining ingredients and reduce heat to low. Cook 10 minutes, stirring occasionally. Remove from heat and let cool completely, about 30 minutes.

④ Pour the mixture into a food processor and process until smooth.

LEMON BUTTER

3 tablespoons butter, divided

1 medium shallot, finely chopped

¼ cup dry white wine such as Sancerre, sauvignon blanc, or pinot grigio

2 tablespoons fresh lemon juice

2 tablespoons heavy cream

Pinch of kosher salt

① In a small saucepan, melt 1 tablespoon of the butter over medium-high heat, then add the chopped shallot and cook, stirring until soft, about 2 minutes. Add the wine and lemon juice and heat 1 additional minute.

② Add the cream and salt and stir to combine. Remove from heat and stir in the remaining butter. Serve warm.

A.C.G. BUTTER

2 teaspoons capers, rinsed, drained, and patted dry

2 tablespoons anchovies

1 tablespoon extra virgin olive oil

2 garlic cloves

1 cup (2 sticks) cold unsalted butter, sliced into chunks

½ teaspoon kosher salt

¼ teaspoon freshly ground black pepper

① In a small saucepan, combine the capers, anchovies, olive oil, and garlic and cook over medium heat, stirring often, until the mixture begins to brown, about 3 minutes. Remove from heat and let cool for 5 minutes.

② Place the caper mixture, butter, salt, and pepper to a food processor and process until smooth.

ROSEMARY AND GARLIC BUTTER

3 garlic cloves

1 cup (2 sticks) cold unsalted butter, sliced into chunks

2 tablespoons fresh rosemary, chopped

1 teaspoon kosher salt

½ teaspoon freshly ground black pepper

① Place all the ingredients in a food processor and process until smooth.

BASIC HOMEMADE BREADCRUMBS

Fresh or stale (but not rock-hard) bread

① "If you're using fresh bread, before proceeding to step 2, cut bread into slices and place on an ungreased cookie sheet. Bake in a 300° F oven for 15 minutes, then let cool.

② Cut the bread into 2-inch chunks and place in a food processor, working in batches if necessary. Process until crumbs are about the size of grains of rice. Alternatively, you can place the bread chunks in a resealable plastic bag and roll a rolling pin over it until the breadcrumbs reach the desired size.

③ Store in an airtight container in the refrigerator for up to 1 month.

PANKO BREADCRUMBS

For panko breadcrumbs, follow the recipe for Basic Homemade Breadcrumbs (above), but use white bread only and remove all crust from the bread first.

ITALIAN-SEASONED BREADCRUMBS

1 cup Basic Homemade Breadcrumbs (page 142)

½ teaspoon dried parsley

¼ teaspoon dried oregano

¼ teaspoon dried basil

⅛ teaspoon garlic powder

① Mix all the ingredients together until thoroughly combined.

TOASTED BREADCRUMBS

1 tablespoon extra virgin olive oil, divided

1 large garlic clove, minced

1 teaspoon lemon zest

1 cup Basic Homemade Breadcrumbs (page 142)

¾ tablespoon chopped Italian flat-leaf parsley

1 teaspoon kosher salt

½ teaspoon freshly ground black pepper

① In a small skillet, heat ½ tablespoon of the olive oil over medium heat. Add the garlic and cook, stirring until soft, about 1–2 minutes. Add the lemon zest and cook until fragrant, about 30 seconds.

② Add the breadcrumbs, parsley, salt, pepper, and remaining olive oil. Remove from heat and stir until well combined.

QUICK-REFERENCE COOKING CHART

This table is a good jumping-off point for selecting the basic time and temperature setting for your air fryer. Since ingredients differ in size, shape, and brand, these are guidelines only, so experiment to find what works best for your ingredients.

INGREDIENT	QUANTITY	TEMP (°F)	TIME (MIN)	NOTES
MEAT, POULTRY AND FISH				
Baby back pork ribs	½ slab	360	30	rub with oil and seasoning; stand in basket
Bacon	4 slices, halved	370	15	flip halfway through
Chicken, bone-in	2 pieces	370	25	spray with oil; flip halfway through
Chicken, boneless, breaded	4 pieces	380	10	spray with oil; flip halfway through
Chicken wings	8 wings	400	25	toss with oil and season; shake 2 times
Fish fillet	2–4 ounces	370	10	spray with oil; flip halfway through
Hamburger	2 4-ounce patties	360	7–14	flip halfway through
Hot dogs/Sausages	4–6 links	380	10–14	flip halfway through
Pork chops	2 chops, 4–6 ounces each	350	14–18	rub with oil and seasoning; flip halfway through
Rack of lamb	4–6 ribs	350	15–20	rub with oil and seasoning
Steak	2 steaks, 4–6 ounces each	360	8–12	rub with oil and salt; flip halfway through

INGREDIENT	QUANTITY	TEMP (°F)	TIME (MIN)	NOTES
VEGETABLES				
Cauliflower	1 head	350	15	rub with oil and seasoning; add 1 cup of water in the heating chamber
Eggplant	1–2 cups	350	15	toss in oil and seasoning; shake 2 times
French fries, fresh-cut	1 cup	400	14	toss with oil; shake 2 times
Green beans	2 cups	350	12	shake 2 times
Peppers, small	6 peppers	400	12	shake 2 times
Squash and zucchini	1–2 cups	350	15	toss in oil and seasoning; shake 2 times
Sweet potato fries, fresh-cut	1 cup	400	14	toss with oil; shake 2 times
Tomatoes, grape or cherry	1 pint	370	10–12	toss in oil; shake 2 times
Tomatoes, roma	3	350	10	halve; toss in oil with salt
FROZEN FOODS				
Cheese sticks	6–8 pieces	400	8	shake once
Chicken fingers	4 pieces	400	12	flip halfway through
Chicken, fried	2 pieces	370	20	flip halfway through
Chicken nuggets	1–2 cups	400	12	shake 2 times
Chicken wings, pre-cooked	8 wings	400	20	shake 2 times
Fish sticks	8 pieces	400	10–12	shake 2 times
French fries, crinkle-cut or thick	1–2 cups	400	12	spray with oil; shake 2 times
French fries, thin	1–2 cups	400	10	spray with oil; shake 2 times
Spring rolls	4 rolls	400	8–10	spray with oil; shake once
Sweet-potato fries	1–2 cups	400	12–14	spray with oil; shake 2 times
Tater tots	1–2 cups	400	12	shake 2 times

INDEX